COMPLEX LITIGATION—A PRACTICAL GUIDE TO CASE MANAGEMENT AND DECISION MAKING

Don G. Rushing

Wolters Kluwer

Published by Wolters Kluwer in New York.

Wolters Kluwer Legal & Regulatory U.S. serves customers worldwide with CCH and Kluwer Law International products.

Printed in the United States of America

ISBN 978-1-5438-8351-0

About Wolters Kluwer Legal & Regulatory U.S.

Wolters Kluwer Legal & Regulatory U.S. delivers expert content and solutions in the areas of law, corporate compliance, health compliance, and reimbursement. Its practical solutions help customers successfully navigate the demands of a changing environment to drive their daily activities, enhance decision quality and inspire confident outcomes.

Serving customers worldwide, its legal and regulatory portfolio includes products under the CCH Incorporated, Kluwer Law International, ftwilliam.com and MediRegs names. They are regarded as exceptional and trusted resources for general legal and practice-specific knowledge, compliance and risk management, dynamic workflow solutions, and expert commentary.

WOLTERS KLUWER SUPPLEMENT NOTICE

This product is updated on a periodic basis with supplements and/or new editions to reflect important changes in the subject matter.

If you are interested in subscribing to this content digitally via our VitalLaw platform, please call 1-800-638-8437.

Important Contact Information

- To order any title, go to *https://law-store.wolterskluwer.com/* or call 1-800-638-8437.
- To subscribe to this content digitally via our VitalLaw platform, please call 1-800-638-8437.
- To contact Customer Service, e-mail *customer.service@wolterskluwer .com* or call 1-800-234-1660.
- To review your account history or pay an invoice online, visit *www.WoltersKluwerLR.com/payinvoices.*

Wolters Kluwer

For Cindy, my wife of many years, for her encouragement to write this book.

ABOUT THE AUTHOR

Don G. Rushing
Retired Partner, Morrison & Foerster, LLP

Don Rushing is an experienced law firm leader, trial lawyer, and recognized authority on bet-the-company litigation.

Mr. Rushing has served in many roles as a law firm leader over his long career, including Managing Partner of Gray, Cary, Ames & Frye, Co-Chair and CEO of Gray Cary Ware & Freidenrich, Chair of Gray Cary's litigation department, Co-Chair of Morrison & Foerster's global litigation department, and Chair of Morrison & Foerster's chairperson selection committee.

As an experienced trial lawyer who is a Fellow of the American College of Trial Lawyers, Associate of the American Board of Trial Advocates, and Certified Civil Trial Advocate of the National Board of Trial Advocacy, Mr. Rushing enjoys a well-deserved reputation for successfully trying complex cases for his clients. Equipped with an M.B.A. in Business Economics and Finance, Mr. Rushing understands the business realities that companies face. This enables him to develop case strategies that align with clients' business goals. As an Air Force Academy graduate, pilot, and former Air Force officer who served in the Air Force

Systems Command research and development community, he provides technically informed legal advice in complex litigation.

Mr. Rushing has served as national coordinating and trial counsel for companies in mass disaster, serial tort, toxic tort, and consumer product matters that involved class action, multi-jurisdiction, and multi-district proceedings in more than 25 states and five foreign jurisdictions. His varied industry experience spans companies in the aerospace, technology, transportation, chemical and applied materials, consumer products, financial services, and mining sectors. He has tried or arbitrated over 70 cases to conclusion in his 45-year career.

Mr. Rushing has been recognized by several top publications for his expertise in commercial litigation, with particular emphasis on aviation and product liability litigation. Mr. Rushing has been ranked as a leading aviation lawyer by *Chambers*, *Legal 500 US*, *Benchmark Litigation*, and *Euromoney's Expert Guides*. Mr. Rushing also has received recognition from *The Best Lawyers in America* in the fields of bet-the-company, commercial, and product liability litigation and from *Southern California Super Lawyers* in class action and mass tort litigation. In 2010, *Daily Journal* recognized him as one of California's "Top 100" leading lawyers. *Best Lawyers* named him "San Diego Product Liability Lawyer of the Year" in 2013 and "San Diego Bet-the-Company Litigator of the Year" in 2015, and *SD Metro Magazine* named him one of San Diego's Top 25 Attorneys. For 35 years, Martindale-Hubbell has rated him "AV Preeminent."

Mr. Rushing received his B.S. in 1970 from the U.S. Air Force Academy, his M.B.A. in 1973 from the University of Southern California, and his J.D. in 1978 from the University of California at Los Angeles School of Law. During law school, Mr. Rushing was a member of the *UCLA Law Review* editorial board.

From 1970 to 1975, Mr. Rushing served as an officer with the U.S. Air Force Systems Command's Space and Missile Systems Organization, where he was awarded the Air Force Commendation Medal for work in the Advanced Ballistic Reentry Systems program. He is a graduate of the U.S. Army Airborne School, and holds an Airborne rating.

TABLE OF CONTENTS

A complete table of contents for each chapter is included at the beginning of the chapter.

ACKNOWLEDGMENTS

"If I have seen further it is by standing on the shoulders of Giants."

—Sir Isaac Newton

I have my friends Malcolm Wheeler and Scott Barker of Wheeler Trigg O'Donnell to thank for the origins of this book. For many years, I taught a variety of trial advocacy topics for my law firms, the National Institute of Trial Advocacy, the Louis M. Welsh Chapter of the American Inns of Court, the University of San Diego School of Law, at symposia, and for other law firms. When I retired from the full-time practice of law and began sorting through notebooks of material containing these presentations to decide what to throw away and what to keep, my wife Cindy suggested I consider sharing some of what I learned on these topics with a broader audience; a series of articles or a book to serve as a vessel for the transfer of human capital to other generations of trial lawyers. I put together an outline containing the typical topics one would cover in a trial advocacy class and sent it off to Mal and Scott for comment. They not only are brilliant lawyers but extraordinarily kind human beings, and they let me down gently. Their message was candid—this has been done before and done well. They also were encouraging—the last two chapters on case management and litigation decision making had not been comprehensively written about before and were worthy of a book. Out of their encouragement sprang the concept for this book. I am deeply grateful to them for their support and critique of the book as it developed.

As a young lawyer, I've benefited greatly from the mentorship of senior trial lawyers like the late Hon. Rudi M. Brewster and David E. Monahan who were not only outstanding trial lawyers but excellent teachers. The opportunity to try cases with gifted trial lawyers like the Hon. William McCurine, to teach with many gifted instructors like James Brosnahan, Julie Matloff Kennedy, Jordan Eth, Michael Jacobs, David Walsh, and Henry Brown when I was a partner with Morrison & Foerster also helped shape this text.

This book owes much to opportunities to collaborate with gifted lawyers in the management of cases. Thomas L. Sager, former Senior Vice President & General Counsel of DuPont, was a leader in creating techniques for efficient case development and the formation of collaborative work teams through the DuPont Primary Law Firm Network. I was privileged to participate in those efforts for over a decade, and have borrowed many of the practices developed by the DuPont Law Department in writing about client communications and case management. Over many cases in our work together, I also observed and collaborated with Thomas P. Schult of Berkowitz Oliver, a master in client communications and sound decision making, and am a better lawyer for it.

Several people read and commented upon various sections of this book. Their reviews were most helpful to me. Special thanks to Dr. Anne Marie Welsh, the "Book Doctor" and an excellent developmental editor, for her help in shaping the text. Thanks to Mal Wheeler, Scott Barker, George R. McFall, Edward V. Brennan, Professors Linda Lane and Kimberly Gosling of the University of San Diego School of Law, two of my mentees and former Morrison & Foerster colleagues, William B. Sailer, former Senior Vice President & Legal Counsel of Qualcomm Inc., my classmate Lt. Gen. (Ret.) Tome Walters, and Dr. John E. Scarborough, President of Litigation Analytics, Inc., for reading and commenting on various chapters of the book.

Special thanks to Edmond Stoops, President of Litigation Art and Science, my trial consultant in many cases, who combined his theater training and technology savvy to assist our trial teams to bring their cases to life in the courtroom. He applied his thoughtfulness and creativity to help prepare the figures and illustrations in this book.

INTRODUCTION

"Learn from the mistakes of others. You can't live long enough to make them all yourself."

—Eleanor Roosevelt

Complex Litigation—A Practical Guide to Case Management and Decision Making is a practical guide for lawyers responsible for complex litigation, those aspiring to that role, and in-house counsel and insurers responsible for overseeing the efforts of outside litigation counsel. I write from a civil litigation defense perspective, though the lessons discussed here apply equally to both sides of litigation and to both civil and criminal cases.

By complex litigation, I mean cases—or more frequently families of cases—involving multiple lawsuits, parties, jurisdictions, claims, and defenses, large numbers of fact witnesses, documents, and experts, and extensive pretrial motion practice.[1] These cases invariably require teams of lawyers, often from more than one law firm, working closely with their clients and cooperating with each other in the common enterprise of case strategy development and execution.

Complex litigation may be distinguished from simpler single plaintiff, single defendant, single cause of action civil cases, or single defendant criminal cases involving straightforward charging allegations

[1] Federal Judicial Center's *Manual for Complex Litigation (Fourth)* (2004) does not directly define what is meant by "complex litigation." Instead, the manual describes the roles and responsibilities of the court and counsel in managing cases deemed by the court to require treatment as a complex case. California Rule of Court 3.400 offers a question-begging definition of a "complex case" as an action that "requires exceptional judicial management to avoid placing unnecessary burdens on the court or the litigants and to expedite the case, keep costs reasonable, and promote effective decision making by the court, the parties, and counsel." The rule then goes on to list several factors that a court may look to in determining whether an action is a "complex case," including the potential for numerous pretrial motions raising difficult or novel legal issues, large numbers of witnesses and documents, numerous separately represented parties, coordination with related actions pending in other courts, and the potential for substantial post-judgment judicial supervision.

because it demands a "complex systems" perspective. By that, I mean a view of your case that appreciates the highly contingent, multi-determinate nature of the process you are engaged in. Examples of "complex systems" include the climate, the economy, and social networks. While not as complex as these examples, big case litigation shares many of the attributes of this type of process because it involves many actors who can behave in chaotic and unpredictable ways interacting with each other in an interdependent way.

For this reason, the observations I offer are principles to be applied to the different circumstances presented in a particular litigation you may be asked to lead. I will urge you to look for patterns, because each case of this type is unique in the facts, applicable law, and human dynamics involved, but exhibits common attributes. I will suggest you look for the unexpected emergent behaviors that arise from seemingly simple interactions and that affect the flow of the litigation. I will suggest questions that you should be asking of yourself and your team as you proceed through the complex litigation process. We assess a situation based on our questions about it. Ask the right question and the hope is for a "right answer." Ask the wrong questions, or fail to ask questions at all, and you abandon all hope of getting to a sound answer.[2]

I've been a practicing trial lawyer for over 45 years, and for much of my practice I served as national coordinating and trial counsel for companies facing the proverbial "bet the company" case. Many of those cases involved mass tort, serial tort, and class action litigation over multiple jurisdictions, most domestic and some foreign. Frequently, the cases were managed through multi-district litigation or coordination procedures. I often had the opportunity to work with lawyers from my own firm, with talented local counsel in jurisdictions around the United States and abroad, and with consultants and experts in all manner of scientific, engineering, medical, and economic disciplines in a coordinated effort to protect the client's interests. Many of the cases involved multiple plaintiffs and multiple defendants, with crossclaims flying in all directions. The professional relationships that developed with lawyers on all sides of the cases often ripened into personal relationships of lasting value. The practice of law, even in the pressure-filled circumstances of complex litigation, still can be conducted in a polite, respectful, and cooperative manner.

---

[2] Werner Heisenberg, the famous German physicist, said that "We have to remember that what we observe is not nature in itself but the nature exposed to our method of questioning."

Along the way, I've picked up some lessons in complex case management, team leadership, and ligation decision making—on occasion by doing it the wrong way and frequently by watching and listening to mentors, co-counsel, and opponents—that I hope to pass along to you in this book. You've reached this point in your legal career after a great deal of hard work and hard-earned experience. Your personal goal in getting to this point was to be the right person, ready to seize the right opportunity, at the right time when a client calls. You will draw on all your experience to create a vision of what a successful result for your client will be, for what's required to achieve it, and how to communicate that clearly to your team. The pointers contained in the following chapters are designed to help equip you to meet that challenge.

This book does not explore the essential courtroom skills necessary to deliver winning results. There are many books telling the advocate how to prepare for and try a case, some of them excellent[3]—I cannot do better.

Nor is this book intended as a primer on various procedural tools often employed in complex litigation such as applications for designation of families of cases for multi-district litigation treatment, *forum non conveniens* motions, removal petitions, or motions challenging jurisdiction or choice of venue.[4] While these tools frequently serve as important means to accomplish tactical objectives in cases, they are not within the scope of this book.

All of us are familiar with the case study method we used in law school. I employ a variation of that method at points in the book to illustrate the points I make. We learn best from examples and, while

---

[3] *See, e.g.*, Michael E. Tigar, *Examining Witnesses* (2nd ed. 2004); Michael E. Tigar, *Persuasion: The Litigator's Art* (1999); Irving Younger, *The Advocate's Deskbook: The Essentials of Trying a Case* (1988); Gerry Spence, *How to Argue and Win Every Time* (1995); Stephen Lubet, *Modern Trial Advocacy—Analysis and Practice* (2nd ed. 1997); Keith Evans, *Common Sense Rules of Advocacy for Lawyers* (2004).

[4] *See, e.g.*, Hon. John F. Nangle, *From the Horse's Mouth: The Workings of the Judicial Panel on Multidistrict Litigation*, 66 Def. Couns. J. 341 (1999) (explaining the workings of the Judicial Panel on Multidistrict Litigation in deciding whether cases filed in multiple jurisdictions requires MDL treatment); Don G. Rushing & Ellen N. Adler, *Some Inconvenient Truths About Forum Non Conveniens Law in International Aviation Disasters*, 74 J. Air Law &d Com. 403 (2009) (provides a primer on *forum non conveniens* procedures); David E. Steinberg, *Motion to Transfer and the Interests of Justice*, 66 Notre Dame Law Rev. 443 (1999). A book detailing various procedures useful in complex litigation is Jay Tidmarsh & Roger H. Trandsrud, *Complex Litigation and Its Alternatives* (Foundation Press 2002).

protecting client confidences, I provide stories intended to demonstrate a particular learning point. I also use examples from leadership, management, and decision-making literature to hopefully enrich the discussion.

Chapter 1 opens with a discussion of the importance of understanding client objectives and priorities and aligning litigation strategy with those objectives. You will also find techniques to aid you in gaining a clear understanding of the answer to the question: What is my assignment? I also discuss tools to aid in clarity of client communications and gain that all important early alignment between client and counsel about potential case outcomes, risks and rewards, and litigation costs. I also offer some suggestions to strengthen and preserve your relationship with the client during the case.

Chapter 2 explores a simple premise: The art of the advocate is crafting a good story and telling it effectively so that the listener prefers your story over that of your opponent. I will explore the reasons why the use of the story form is central to persuasion, as well as the elements of a good story, how those are developed in litigation, and methods to assess the potency of a story. The task of theme and theory identification and the development of the client's story primarily falls on the shoulders of the litigation team leader. The primary skills needed to discharge this responsibility are also discussed. When the contours of the story are not outlined early and honed as the facts are developed, the case drifts. You and your client will not sleep comfortably until you can envision a story to explain the case and see a path to success.

Chapter 3 deals with basic leadership principles that may be applied in leading teams of lawyers engaged in complex litigation. Lawyers generally don't pay much attention to the art of leadership in the conduct of their practices. But leadership skills are extremely important in the successful conduct of complex litigation that invariably involves teams of lawyers, support staff, and experts. Lawyers may not have had leadership opportunities before going to law school, and usually don't receive leadership training as part of their law studies. But leadership skills can be learned, especially those that are necessary to organize, train, motivate, and direct trial teams to accomplish a client's objectives.

Chapter 4 discusses basic management principles that may be used to keep the litigation team organized, aligned in their efforts, efficient in their work, and effective in accomplishing the client's goals. Even though the vast majority of cases filed in our court systems are resolved short of trial, I believe that preparation for trial at the very outset of litigation leads to better, less expensive outcomes for the client. This chapter discusses the "how to" of effective trial preparation, including the preparation of a trial notebook to carry you through trial preparation and trial. The importance of task lists to control teamwork processes is highlighted. I also touch upon the challenge of building collaborative work teams across firm lines to employ the best available resources in solving the client's problems.

Chapter 5 addresses the management of the litigation decision-making process. I focus on common mistakes and pitfalls in decision making that can cause blunders and damage client relationships, how to spot the pitfalls before you step into them, and prescriptions for avoiding mistakes. Several myths regarding the decision-making process are discussed. I also suggest methods to better manage the decision-making process to improve the product of that process.

I conclude in Chapter 6 with a high-level summary of the key "take aways" from the earlier discussion topics. Perfection in complex case management and decision making isn't attainable, but improvement is possible with the application of these lessons.

Before we begin, however, let's address a threshold question: Who decides who the litigation team leader is? I'll start with the lawyerly answer that it depends on the case. And it depends on how the case comes to the lawyer or law firm.

Some trial lawyers enjoy sterling reputations for the ability to successfully handle large, complex cases, and are retained directly by the client or the client's insurer. In this circumstance, the selection of the leader is obvious. This is good work if you can get it.

Some cases involve "beauty contests" where the lawyer or her law firm are invited to compete through an interview process to land the engagement. The ability to get into the competition is no mean feat, and the fielding of a team and creation of a polished presentation are hard work, frequently involving a substantial time commitment. In this situation, the composition of the team and designation of a team leader for the "pitch" usually is done through discussions among the partners and firm management. The choice of a leader won't be clear until the contest is won, though part of the "pitch" inevitably will involve some promises who the lawyer will be that will lead the effort. A frequent question from clients in the litigation counsel selection process is: "Who will give the closing argument?"

Some cases come to one of the firm's lawyers who is not a litigator but who enjoys a relationship of trust with the client. In this situation, the contact lawyer might have a favorite litigator to bring into the case, or might contact firm management and seek guidance about the best available firm resource. The contact lawyer frequently will have a good sense what the client wants in a team leader, what type of background and experience will be most attractive, and what personality will blend best.

And sometimes, a lawyer will just happen to be in the right place at the right time. In my own case, I was fortunate to be mentored as a young lawyer by a remarkably gifted trial lawyer who loved his clients and was loved in return.[5] They trusted him with their most difficult matters. When he went on the federal bench as the capstone to a magnificent career in the courtroom, he left me with several of his cases. When one of the clients had a series of big cases involving the same type of product, I received a call from a somewhat skeptical general counsel. The conversation began with an expression of appreciation for how a couple of cases were handled after the departure of my partner to the bench, an observation that while he knew my partner well, he didn't know much about me, and a request I tell him why I was the right lawyer for the job. Whatever I said must have worked. We enjoyed many years working together. Choosing the leader this way is fortuitous and rare. But lightning does strike from time to time.

Sometimes, the "team leader" is not the lead trial lawyer who will try the case or the national coordinating counsel who will guide the strategy for a series of cases in multiple jurisdictions. A more junior lawyer with administrative and organizational skills might take responsibility for the day-to-day management of the case. This lawyer often will serve as the primary interface between the client and the outside lawyers working on the case, and will "manage up" to the lead trial lawyer.

No matter how a case may come to you as team leader, your success in handling the matter will depend on your ability to effectively communicate with your client, develop a compelling story, lead the team with vision and passion, manage the matter efficiently, and make good judgment calls along the way while skirting decision-making blunders. This book is designed to provide you with some tips on how to get the job done.

My intent in writing about team leadership, case management, and litigation decision making in the context of complex litigation is to make some suggestions about how it can be done effectively. You may want to

---

[5] That lawyer was the Hon. Rudi M. Brewster who was a partner at the San Diego law firm of Gray, Cary, Ames & Frye before going on the bench of the U.S. District Court for the Southern District of California where he served with distinction for many years.

use these chapters as an invitation to a dialog rather than simply as a lecture. I suggest you query and interrogate the text to see what you agree and disagree with. And why. Then you can decide what ideas, processes, and behaviors you want to incorporate into your own practice. Happy reading!

CHAPTER 1

CLIENT COMMUNICATIONS AND RELATIONS

"When you talk, you are only repeating what you already know. But if you listen, you may learn something new."

—The Dalai Lama

Success in complex litigation begins with a thorough understanding of the client's objectives and priorities. This requires active listening, and probing for the pain that comes from problems that require a litigation solution. Active listening requires that you pay attention not only to what the client says, but how they say it. Listen with your ears and your eyes. Listen for the tone of voice that reveals the emotions behind the words. Watch for the body language—the non-verbal cues—that are part of the message.

As a younger lawyer, I sometimes found myself too much in "send" rather than "receive" mode. In the Air Force, we called that the "hot mic" problem; an airplane microphone that is stuck on, in transmit mode, sometimes without the speaker realizing it. I'm now convinced that is a mistake. Ask questions, and let the client do most of the talking. Your purpose is to fully understand what the client is telling you about the facts of the case and about their needs and expectations. Clients won't be ready to hear your proposed solutions until they are sure you've heard and understood what they think the problem is and what their needs are.

§ 1.01 UNDERSTANDING THE CLIENT'S BUSINESS AND LITIGATION OBJECTIVES

Good communication with the client begins with a fundamental understanding of the client's business. This is the context within which the dialog about the client's litigation objectives occurs. I found it helpful, indeed necessary, to invest in the client relationship by doing some "off the clock" research into the industry in which the client operated, the position of the company in that industry, statements the company made to the public in its advertising, in regulatory filings, and on its website, and the products involved in the litigation. There usually is a wealth of information about your client's business, products, and services available on websites and in public filings. Most sophisticated businesses will expect its litigators to have educated themselves about what the company does and how it does it. Sometimes, you will need to not only invest your time in this effort, but your financial resources as well.

As an example, a partner and I were retained in a case involving the crash of a particular type of jet-powered helicopter frequently used in tourist flight operations. Neither of us had flown in the helicopter before, and we felt it important to an understanding of the case to understand the emergency operating procedures potentially involved in the crash. We also felt it inappropriate to charge the client for our familiarization with the product. We hired a flight instructor to take us on a demonstration ride in the same type of helicopter involved in the crash. By spending a couple of hours of our time and several hundred dollars of the firm's money, we were able to observe firsthand how the aircraft operated, how the pilot was to perform the applicable emergency procedures, and even fly the aircraft to gain a sense of how it handled under normal operating conditions. This investment paid dividends for us as the litigation progressed.

The client's expectation that you will understand their business not only applies to long-time counsel for the company, but to law firms competing for the company's business in "beauty contests." Intelligent questions about the company in new business interviews certainly can impress a prospective client, but "tell me about your business" certainly will not. If you are equipped with an understanding of the company's business when you enter the meeting, you will be prepared to ask questions directed to a strategy for the litigation, and to understand the answers you receive.

We are all challenged by the Lockean "problem of language."[1] The words coming out of the client's mouth signify ideas in the mind of the speaker, and may mean something different to her than what you, as the listener, perceive the meaning to be. Close attention to a shared understanding of the meaning of the words used by the client is important. This particularly is so when the discussion moves into technical areas or when industry jargon is in common use.

We also are challenged by what Prof. Elizabeth Loftus refers to as the "misinformation effect."[2] We simply don't always remember accurately the details of a conversation because of new information received after the original conversation. This makes all the more important close listening to the words and body language that accompanies the words, contemporaneous notes about what is said, and perhaps an extra pair of ears and eyes in the form of a colleague who accompanies you to important meetings with the client and who can confirm what you thought you understood the client to be saying. And to ask questions designed to elicit amplification upon what is said. Just as the trial lawyer's easiest question, "what happened next?," keeps the witness talking, questions to your client such as "please tell me more about that" or "tell me why that's important to you" will encourage your client to provide more information. A restatement of your client's responses also aids in understanding; "what I hear you saying is. . . ." A dialog with your client that asks for clarification what the ideas behind the words are and that avoids post-conversation contamination of the message will enhance your ability to communicate clearly and remember and record accurately what is said and meant.

There are several key questions for the client at the outset of the litigation (and periodically throughout the case). I suggest you ask the following questions.

[A] *"What do you want?"*

This simple, open-ended question gives the client the opportunity to tell you the desired outcome of the litigation. The answer allows you to understand the client's objectives, and how realistic the client's

---

[1] John Locke, *An Essay Concerning Human Understanding Book III* (Kenneth P. Winkler ed. 1996).

[2] Elizabeth F. Loftus & Geoffrey R. Loftus, *On the Permanence of Stored Information in the Brain*, 35(5) Am. Psychol. 409–20 (May 1980); Elizabeth F. Loftus, David G. Miller, & Helen J. Burns, *Semantic Integration of Verbal Information into a Visual Memory*, 4(1) J. Exp. Psychol. Hum. Learn. Mem. 19–31 (1978).

expectations are. The answer also will tell you whether you have some work to do in setting reasonable expectations. Initially, it may not be possible to determine what a successful outcome for the client might be because you don't yet have a good grasp of the facts and the law applicable to the dispute. But posing the question at the outset allows you to understand where the client wants to go with the litigation.

Sometimes, the clients won't know what they want because they won't know what is possible. In this event, explain what you think is possible, give the client options to consider, and explain the costs and benefits of each option. In this way, you are helping the client decide what's needed.

[B] *"What does success look like?"*

This question gets at the same issue, the client's litigation objectives, in a slightly more nuanced way. You may be surprised at the answer to this question. The client may not tell you they want a clear win in the litigation. You may hear instead that they want a quick way out of the lawsuit in a settlement, a way of keeping an important product on the market, an approach to the litigation that will deter suits by others on the same subject, or the ability to continue using their intellectual property free from further claims. Whatever the response, it is important to fully understand what a "win" looks like in your client's eyes.

I've had clients, for example, tell me (and mean it) that they will litigate a particular type of case through trial and appeal in each individual matter, as expensive and time consuming as that will be, because the long-term health of the company demands it. I've also had them tell me they simply want the case to go away because it is a needless distraction from the company's business interests and they do not wish to spend the money necessary to adequately defend the claim. But you won't know the client's priorities until you ask. Sometimes, your client might not know what a successful result would look like. At an early stage in the litigation, you might not either. In that event, you may need to say: "Let's go on that journey together."

[C] *"What are the financial concerns?"*

Litigation costs may be an important consideration for companies or business units with limited revenues. A *The New Yorker* magazine cartoon cleverly captured the issue. The cartoon depicts a lawyer sitting across a desk from a client. The caption has the lawyer telling the client he has a good case, and then asking how much justice he can afford.[3] Just so.

And even when a company well can afford the legal expenses associated with litigation, other ways of spending that money may be more appealing. The client may not be in a position to fully answer the question concerning litigation costs until in-house counsel sees a budget for the litigation prepared by retained counsel and assesses the potential impacts of the litigation on the company's operations.

The setting of underwriting reserves by company insurers may be a concern because of increased insurance costs in future years. Insurers may also have the right to control the litigation under the applicable contract of insurance, and may deem it more expeditious and cost-effective to settle a claim rather than litigate it, even over the insured's objections. Involving the insurer in a tripartite discussion of the client's litigation objectives at the appropriate time will aid in setting objectives and designing a litigation strategy to meet those objectives.

Required financial disclosures under Financial Accounting Standards Board rules for loss contingencies must also be taken into account. Formerly known as FAS No. 5 and now known by the unwieldy title of FASB Accounting Standard Condition (ASC) subtopic 450-20 Contingencies: Loss Contingency, this rule requires formal disclosure by public companies of an "existing condition, situation, or set of circumstances involving uncertainty as to possible gain or loss to an entity that will ultimately be resolved when one or more future events occur or fail to occur."[4] Disclosures of this type, when required, may have a direct impact upon share prices. And they are rife with concerns about loss of confidentiality concerning the company's litigation posture and approach. When these issues appear, I would advise that the Chief Financial Officer and the company's outside auditors be involved in the discussion. Trial lawyers well understand the vagaries of litigation and concerns for confidentiality of their advice to the client, but may not be able to comment authoritatively on issues of accounting materiality and required financial disclosures. Discussion with the client at an early stage of the case about the possibility of such a financial reporting requirement is helpful in framing the financial consequences of litigation.

---

[3] *The New Yorker Book of Lawyer Cartoons* 73 (1993).

[4] Financial Accounting Standards Board Accounting Standard Condition subtopic 450-20.

[D] *"What are the operational concerns?"*

Litigation frequently not only requires the attention of a company's legal department, but other employees who participated in some way in the activities that are the subject of the litigation. A company director, officer, or employee may have been involved in a transaction at the core of the dispute. Or responsible for a product's design, development, and production. Or part of a marketing effort for a service by the company. Or the invention of a technology that was awarded a patent. The possibilities are virtually endless. Litigation almost inevitably will prove to be a distraction for some employees from the central business of the company. This diversion of company resources and personnel will be necessary to find and produce documents, provide important background on the matter, serve as in-house experts, and provide deposition and trial testimony. This is a "hidden" cost of litigation that doesn't appear in the typical litigation budget, but nonetheless is a cost that the client and trial team must take into consideration in devising a litigation strategy.

But the operational costs are not just financial in nature. Pending lawsuits also may have an adverse impact on employee morale. Employees critical to the company's day-to-day operations often are required to serve as key witnesses in litigation. Time away from their "day job" to prepare for and attend depositions, hearings, and trials imposes additional burdens, and adds to the stress of their job. In my own experience in serial litigation over a product involved in multiple wrongful death and personal injury cases and filed in state and federal courts around the United States, one company engineer was deposed twelve times (despite requests for protective orders) and testified for his company in four different trials. He was a superb witness and a conscientious employee, but this added burden took its toll on him emotionally and physically. He was diverted from his work as a talented engineer, a job he loved, to serve as a critical company witness concerning the development, testing, and use of the company's product, a role he disliked but was quite good at. While hard to quantify, this "cost" is real and should be reckoned with in the preparation of a litigation strategy.

Potential reputational harm from the mere filing of a suit or from information that may come to light during discovery or trial also should be considered. Is damage to the company's brand a possibility? If so, how might that damage be mitigated? If adverse publicity results, what is the potential that a local, state, or federal regulatory agency will become interested in the issue, to the disadvantage of the client? And will the prosecution or defense of the suit potentially trigger additional suits by other groups of plaintiffs, compounding the problems associated with the initial suit?

One of the many roles outside litigation counsel, and particularly national trial and coordinating counsel, plays is as a sounding board for the client in discerning whether it should seek exoneration in the courtroom or peace through a settlement.

[E] *"What are the trade-offs?"*

This question asks the client to value various possible outcomes in the litigation, considering anticipated transactional costs, potential diversion of company resources to the suit, impacts on customer or supply chain partners, and effects on the company's brand. The answer to this question gives the trial team some insight into the client's priorities as they set in place a litigation plan. The answer also allows the team to look for "win-win" solutions with an opponent that may not have been obvious until the client describes the relative importance and weight to be given to costs and impacts of the litigation.

§ 1.02 MANAGING CLIENT EXPECTATIONS

Whether the client says so or not, the C Suite's point of view is very likely to be: "Don't let the litigation tail wag the business dog." However important the case may be to you, it's just one of many big or bigger problems that the occupants of the C Suite must juggle. A trial lawyer who has sat in a company board meeting waiting to brief the directors on a pending case will be struck by the breadth, complexity, and importance of other matters before the board. Understand that clients make products and provide services for profit; they don't litigate for fun. Businesses are responsible to directors and shareholders to maximize the firm's value. Businesses are obligated to protect the market integrity of their products and service offerings. Your goal as the litigation team leader is to help your client discharge these responsibilities.

At the outset of litigation, candid discussion with the client about what is possible and what is not will be vital to a good client relationship during the case. The client should understand that creating achievable goals and effectively implementing them in the litigation will be best for the company in the long run.

A word on litigation strategy discussions in so-called "beauty contests." While it is tempting to make promises in business pitches that will entice the client to hire you as their lawyer, you are much better off creating credibility with the client with your candor and setting expectations that can be met. Over-promising and under-delivering is not a formula for success. If the client recognizes that your statements about the case are unrealistically optimistic, you won't get the representation. If the client senses that the team pitching the case isn't the team that will be doing the work as the litigation progresses, you won't get the case. And if a client has unrealistic expectations at the outset of a case, it is better to know that and to either recalibrate expectations or pass on the representation.

When communicating about a case, whether during an interview for a representation or during the litigation, pay attention to the "voice" you are using. Clients want dispassionate advice, but they also want passionate advocacy and a clear strategy. Make sure you give the client clear signals what "voice" you are using when you communicate; their dispassionate advisor or their passionate advocate with a plan to win.

Clients have a dozen key value drivers that national coordinating and trial counsel must appreciate. Call them the "dirty dozen." Clients want to:

- Avoid damage to brand and market perception.
- Avoid adverse precedent created by case resolution.
- Avoid harm to business relationships.
- Avoid workplace disruption.
- Avoid adverse publicity.
- Avoid regulatory action.
- Avoid legislative action.
- Avoid new suits by opposing counsel.
- Avoid litigation costs.
- Protect employees.
- Time case resolution advantageously.
- Protect intellectual property.

As best you can, place yourself in the client's shoes when you consider how the handling of the litigation might affect each of these challenges. Aim for a thoughtful discussion about the client's priorities among these concerns.

I also suggest you leave room for doubt. Yes, doubt. One of my partners used to tell his clients: "I'm sometimes wrong, but I'm never in doubt!" He was joking, of course. He exercised a healthy skepticism about what the law appeared to be on a particular point and how it might change, whether documents could be read and understood in different ways, what witnesses had to say and whether they could be believed, and whether a particular line of argument would be persuasive. Doubt can be a good thing, because it allows you to discover with your client what the facts are, what helpful perspectives on those facts might be, and how those facts can be sorted honestly into a compelling story for your client.

I suggest you also leave room for healthy disagreement. You won't always agree with the approach advocated by your client or by other members of your litigation team, but you do need to be comfortable with the give-and-take offered by different perspectives on a problem. As the team leader, it is quite important that you not prematurely foreclose discussion that surfaces different perspectives. Signal openness to other ideas.

§ 1.03 SETTING CLIENT COMMUNICATION PATTERNS

Clients want to stay informed about the status of the case. But clients have differing tolerances for the frequency of updates and amount of detail they are given about their matter. I suggest you ask what your client wants, how frequently she wants it, and in what form.

[A] *"Who do we report to?"*

If your client is a corporate entity, you likely will have one or more primary points of contact who have responsibility for the litigation. There may be an associate general counsel who reports to the general counsel who in turn reports to the CEO who is responsible to the board. Or the matter may be of sufficient concern to the company that your reporting may be directly to the general counsel or CFO.

[B] *"Who are the key in-house decision makers?"*

In cases where the general counsel or one of her associates maintains close control over access to business unit employees, you may not have direct access to the ultimate decision makers or to those with information about the facts of the case. But you should at least strive to understand who they are and what they are being told about the litigation. If you work collaboratively with in-house counsel to shape the communications to the decision makers, this will encourage clear communication within the client organization.

[C] *"Who do we communicate with on each issue, and who gets copied?"*

The answer to this question will tell you who to address your phone calls, emails, and case reports to, and who to keep in the information loop in that process. The answer also will give insight into who within the company likely will be involved in decision-making processes as the litigation unfolds.

[D] *"What is the means and frequency of communication preferred by the client?"*

Does the client prefer periodic conference calls or Zoom calls? Are face-to-face formal briefings desired? Are periodic reports required? And if so, is there a format the client prefers counsel to use.

Because modern communication with in-house counsel and insurers may be primarily through e-mail, a word concerning e-mail etiquette is in order. Your objective in writing e-mail updates is to make your communications easy to read, easy to digest, and as brief as possible.

Start in the subject line with "CONFIDENTIAL" to clearly label the email as attorney work product protected or attorney client privileged. Then show the case name associated with email (*e.g.*, "Smith v. Jones") followed by a brief subject (*e.g.*, "Pretrial Order Draft"). This allows the recipient to know what matter and what subject your email addresses. This method also makes filing of the emails in a place where they can be found later much easier for the client.

At the beginning of the body of the email, again indicate the confidentiality of the communication and the applicable privilege or protection. Start with a brief description of what the email is about and any requests for action on the part of the client. Deadlines, such as requested dates by which you want input from the client or last days, should be flagged in red. As an example, the body of your email might begin:

FIGURE 1-1

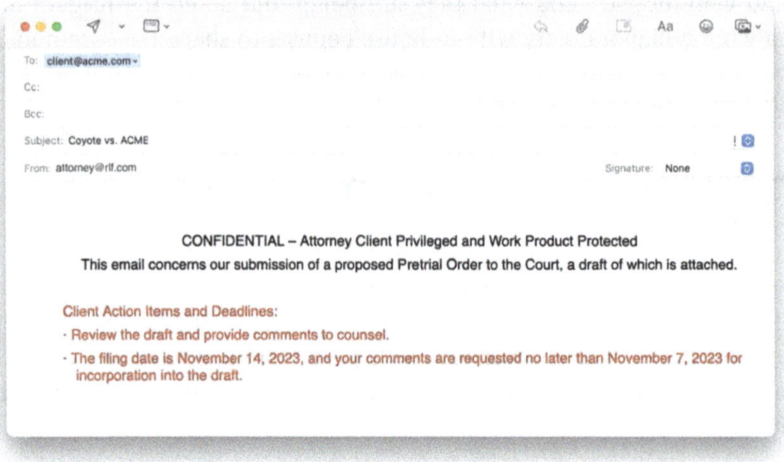

Follow your introduction with a brief summary that includes your recommendations and any key points to be considered by the client. A brief statement of relevant facts and law should follow. Finally, provide a discussion of your recommended action and any alternatives. In drafting emails to a client, I tried to give a clear recommendation before moving to a discussion of possible alternatives. As the bad old lawyer joke goes, clients like a one-armed lawyer who won't constantly say "on the other hand."

Reports differ for various levels of responsibility within the company. The GC may want a few bullet points to report to the Board of Directors or a PowerPoint® slide or two that summarizes the case, but the lawyer managing the day-to-day litigation may need in depth reporting of developments as they occur. Sometimes, the client's Board of Directors or insurance underwriters may request a full case briefing. As an example, in a mass disaster involving a company in the airline industry, the Board of Directors dedicated a full hour to a discussion of the litigation in an off-site meeting. The company's insurers were briefed on the status of the cases on multiple occasions, always in person and with a supporting status report and a PowerPoint® presentation. The time and detail involved in the preparation for these reports will vary according to the client's needs, the audience you will be addressing, and the client's preferred format for the communications.

§ 1.04 INITIAL CRISIS MANAGEMENT AND PUBLIC MESSAGING

If the litigation stems from a mass disaster, a product failure affecting many units and potential harm to humans or the environment, or an exposure to chemicals put into the environment by a company's operations, a quick response is critical. (There may be other circumstances as well, but those certainly are at the top of the list.) An early message talking candidly about what is then known about the problem and what the company is doing in response is an important first step.[5]

Let's turn to media and regulatory agency relations, as these are an important aspects of high-stakes litigation. Companies typically have public relations personnel on staff or on retainer that you must closely coordinate with. Early alignment on a media relations strategy is imperative. What are the risks of a "no comment, litigation is pending" approach? One obvious risk it that you surrender the opportunity to state your client's side of the case and cede this opportunity to your opponent. What is the story we wish to tell, the position we wish to take? I'll talk at length in the next chapter about the potency of the story form in litigation. But the client's interests generally are best served by telling its story powerfully and consistently from the outset of litigation. Who will be responsible for interfacing with the media? Will it be the litigation team leader, a member of the company's public relations staff, or a retained communications firm? In any event, the person responsible for media relations should closely coordinate with the litigation team leader in messaging about the case so that communications are accurate, consistent with an agreed litigation strategy, emphasize the client's themes, and do not reveal confidential information.

In some instances, the litigation may involve a regulatory agency. Accidents involving consumer products may require filings with the Consumer Product Safety Commission. Air, rail, maritime, or trucking accidents involving deaths usually will be investigated by the National Transportation Safety Board or its delegate and may involve standard setting and enforcement agencies such as the Federal Aviation

[5] Norman R. Augustine, *Managing the Crisis You Tried to Prevent*, Harvard Business Review (November/December 1995).

Administration or the National Highway Traffic Safety Administration. Toxic substance spills or releases may involve the U.S. Environmental Protection Administration or a state counterpart. Securities fraud actions may attract the attention of the Securities Exchange Commission and invite enforcement actions by the commission. In a highly regulated society such as ours, management of the involved (or potentially involved) regulatory agency relationship is an important aspect of your overall litigation strategy.

Your litigation team should include relevant agency expertise. This expertise may be found within the client's staff, within your own law firm, or within another firm or consulting group that specializes in a particular agency's regulatory area. The importance of effective interface with regulatory agencies cannot be overstated. This is not an area conducive to learning on the job.

§ 1.05 HELPING CLIENTS UNDERSTAND THE LITIGATION PLAN AND CASE RISKS

[A] Early Case Assessment

A good early case assessment (ECA) sets the initial plan for the case. Within the first 90 days, sooner if possible, develop a proposed case strategy and strategic budget to share with the client. Your initial case strategy should center on the story you intend to tell. Your initial strategic budget should account for the steps you intend to take early in the litigation.

The preparation of an initial plan and budget is a shared responsibility between in-house counsel and retained counsel. The workflow associated with the development of an initial case assessment, sometimes referred to as an early case assessment, can be depicted as follows[6]:

[6] The approach of preparing an early case assessment and strategic budget was pioneered in the 1980s and 1990s by the E.I. DuPont Legal Department under the direction of Vice President and Assistant General Counsel Thomas L. Sager. Thomas L. Sager, Julie S. Mazza, *The Competitive Edge—The Growing Power of the DuPont Legal Model* (4th ed.). The progress of the DuPont Legal Model after the first decade was summarized in DuPont Legal Department, *Leaps & Bounds—Moving Ahead with the DuPont Legal Model* (Crosby Marketing 2001).

FIGURE 1-2

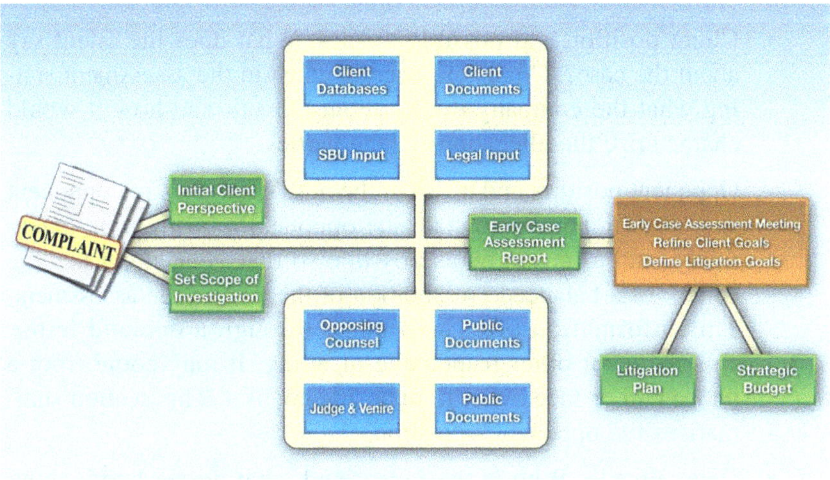

In-house counsel provides the initial client perspective from the strategic business unit (SBU) and legal department, client database search results, and client documents that form the initial client perspective on the litigation as well as the identification of employees within the company with knowledge of the matter. Information gained in initial interviews of key company witnesses by in-house and retained counsel is an important input to an early case assessment.

Retained counsel provides information concerning opposing counsel, the assigned judge, the jury *venire* in jurisdictions where cases are filed, publicly available documents, and press coverage that permits the initial scoping of the investigation. This input should include a brief summary of key aspects of applicable law. Simple jury instructions outlining the various causes of action, defenses, and the elements of proof are a good start. Indeed, they are a critical beginning point for the litigation because they provide the lens through which the facts you develop will be viewed. What facts are relevant to the claims and defenses? What witnesses and documents will be helpful to prove the elements of the causes of action or defenses in the case?

Retained counsel then synthesizes this information into an early (or initial) case assessment that lays out the following key elements:

- Case background. What is the context of the dispute? What are the known facts? This section of your case assessment provides the context for the litigation and the information to follow. This is a brief history of the controversy, and answers the question: "How did we get here?"

- Client position and possible themes. What does the client say about the case? This is the client's voice in the assessment stating what the company thinks about the suit and how it would characterize the allegations of the parties.
- Opponent position and possible themes. What does the opponent say? It is important to state the opponent's position as objectively, and as strongly, as possible so that your client has the benefit of a balanced presentation of the case in the assessment. This information often will come through a demand letter, complaint, or other responsive pleading. It may come from a phone call or meeting with opposing counsel. This section summarizes the opponent's position.
- Court profile. Who is the judge, and what do we know about her? Judges say what the law is and determine how the case will proceed, so her proclivities are an important factor in the litigation. Begin with a judicial profile, and add as you can with information from others about her judicial demeanor, the state of her calendar, and any rulings in similar cases. This section deals with an assessment of the person who will be "calling the balls and strikes."
- Opposing Counsel profile. Who is our opponent and what do we know about him? Describe the firm and lawyers representing your opponent. Provide brief professional profiles, and any information you can develop from others about their reputation for professionalism, honest dealing, and approach to litigation.
- Composition of local jury *venire*. What are the composition and demographics of the venire? Court websites often provide demographic information from the jury commissioner about the population from which a jury will be drawn. Frequently, jury consultants who have done research in a particular jurisdiction can provide additional insight about typical jurors, their attitudes, and their beliefs that are helpful to an initial case evaluation.
- Key witnesses and documents. So far as initially known, who are the important witnesses? What are the key documents?

This is the point in the early case assessment where you will provide a brief summary of the interviews of the key company witnesses you were able to conduct. If the interviews are incomplete, say so and indicate what the importance of the other witnesses may be to the case. Likewise, if you have had the opportunity to review key documents (*e.g.*, a contract, correspondence about a particular event, design specifications, or a securities offering circular), this is the place in your initial case assessment where you will comment on your preliminary observations. Feel comfortable in qualifying your initial impressions of the evidence, because you will not have a complete view of what the witnesses and documents will portray at this early stage.

- Key legal issues. What will the basic jury instructions on key points of law say? Federal and state jurisdictions frequently have pattern jury instructions on the basic points of law governing various types of cases as well as use instructions. Summarize and attach the key jury instructions in this part of your case assessment. The client needs to know, at least preliminarily, what the law is that likely will govern the case.

- Case strengths and weaknesses. What are our best and worst facts, witnesses, and documents? Don't sugar coat this. Be frank about both strengths and weaknesses, so far as they are known at this stage of the case. Lay out the difficult facts, witnesses, and documents. State the good points of your client's case in an objective manner as well. This portion of your case assessment is not the place to engage in chest beating about the strength of the client's case or to minimize potential difficulties you see in the case.

- Client perspective. What does the client want? What is the level of sensitivity of the company to the case? This section contains a summary of the results of your conversations with the client about the company's litigation objectives. The perspective you are feeding back to the client is what you think you heard in initial discussions. This is a further opportunity to gain alignment on the mission you have for the litigation.

- Case evaluation. What does the litigation team think about the potential value of the case in the early stages of the litigation?

This is your best stab at putting a preliminary probability of success on the case, and providing a value for the claims. Of course, you will need in this section to provide some caveats about your initial evaluation of the case. Yes, it is early in the development of the case. Yes, it is difficult to provide a full evaluation until discovery is at least underway, if not completed. Yes, it is a tricky exercise to evaluate a case until you've completed some jury research to determine receptivity to case themes, reactions to witnesses, and values placed upon the case by your mock jury. But the client needs some "going in" probabilities of success and numbers to work with in deciding what to do with the case, and it is your job to provide it—however guarded you may need to be.

- Agreed initial case strategy. What steps should be taken to get from where we are at the start of the case to the winner's circle at the end of the case. This is the place in the case assessment where you provide the broad outlines of a path to victory.[7]

The initial assessment and the beginning strategy contained in it are the "mission" the litigation team sets out to accomplish. The contours of the mission doubtless will change in small ways and large as the case develops or the needs of the client change. The mission must be formally reevaluated on a periodic basis and adapted to the changing circumstances. I will discuss in greater length in Chapter 2 the importance of the use of the story form at all stages of litigation. But an important part of your mission as lead trial counsel will be the early development and continued honing of the story your client will tell throughout the litigation. Without an early statement of your client's theme and story arc, the case will drift and your client will not sleep comfortably.

The draft case assessment should be reviewed with all levels within the company who are directing the litigation and responsible for the result, and with any insurers who have underwriting exposure, the right to control the litigation, or responsibility for fees and costs. Changes

---

[7] The Hon. William Alsup, U.S. District Court for the Northern District of California, referred to this as the "roadmap to victory." More on the importance of this step in Chapter 3—Leadership of the Team when we discuss the need for vision in complex litigation leadership.

should be discussed and adopted to achieve alignment on the initial case strategy, understanding that there inevitably will be changes as the facts are developed or perceptions of the case change. This step is important so that everyone is marching in the same direction with the same understandings and intentions.

The workflow associated with the preparation and vetting of an ECA can be visualized in this way:

FIGURE 1-3

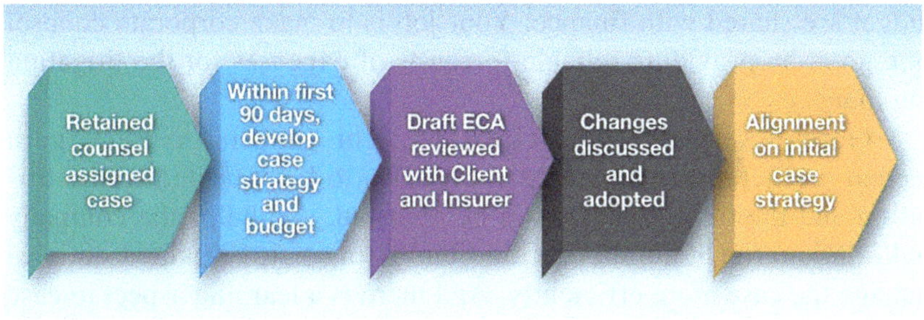

There are four important benefits of initial case assessments: (1) increased client participation in and satisfaction with case planning, (2) alignment of litigation costs with expected outcomes, (3) more efficient and responsive lawyering, and (4) reduced case cycle time (the longer cases continue, the more they cost). A good initial assessment will identify the theme and story line that will be told, outline alternative approaches, establish a starting strategy, and achieve alignment of the goals of the business, the insurer, and retained counsel. This document also will be the foundation for the preparation of a more detailed litigation plan that includes such things as jurisdiction and venue motions, a discovery plan, motions to dismiss or for summary adjudication, and anticipated pretrial motions directed at the exclusion or admission of evidence.

But there also are potential drawbacks to an ECA: It can give you tunnel vision. All the evidence must always be examined for possible significance. You may read a document early in the case and draw a conclusion about its significance. You may read the same document six months into the case and develop a very different impression of its meaning and significance. All team members should be encouraged to question interpretations and conclusions, and to raise doubts about the significance of evidence and the theories that develop from it.

[B] Strategic Budgeting

Accurate forecasting of litigation costs is important to both the client and the law firms involved. In a typical corporate organizational structure, the finance department is answerable to the CEO and Board for the corporate budget. The finance department doesn't want to look bad if unanticipated litigation costs crop up that cause the company to miss its numbers. The corporate counsel function typically is answerable to the finance department for the company's litigation spend and does not want to look bad when litigation expenses that exceed the budget are shared with finance. Your job is to make corporate counsel look good by providing reliable forecasts of expenses for the litigation you manage.

Good case budgeting helps the client (and its insurers) gain needed predictability about the total costs to be expected in the litigation and the timing of costs to be incurred, and helps the company make its quarterly numbers. Good budgeting helps retained counsel manage the case more efficiently. And there is a learning aspect to case budgeting that helps both the business and the outside law firm become more accurate over time in preparing litigation budgets and living within them.

Case budgeting typically uses spreadsheet software. Activities to be costed may use the Uniform Task-Based Billing codes should the client's legal department rely upon them for case review and payment purposes or simply prefer them to alternative approaches to litigation task identification. A spreadsheet may also provide a comparison of budgeted and actual expenses as they are incurred.

A strategic case budget is prepared using phases and categories of activities anticipated in the litigation, staffing of that activity, estimated hours incurred in the performance of the activity, and hourly rates of the assigned staff. These costs are then totaled to present a complete budget. Ideally, retained counsel can not only estimate the total cost of the litigation, but also predict when costs will be incurred in the company's operating quarters so that both the amount and timing of litigation expenses can be anticipated.

This is "ground up" budgeting that is specific to the case, case plan, and client needs. The strategic budget spells out cost estimates for the execution of the plan described in the case assessment. An example of a spreadsheet using this approach is shown below.

FIGURE 1-4

Strategic Case Budget				
Category		Cost		
		Hours	Rate	Amount
L100	**Case Assessment, Development and Administration**			
L110	Fact Investigation/Development			$0
L120	Analysis/Strategy			$0
L130	Experts/Consultants			$0
L140	Document/File Management			$0
L150	Budgeting			$0
L160	Settlement/Non-Binding ADR			$0
L190	Other Case Assessment, Dev. and Admin			$0
L200	**Pre-Trial Pleadings and Motions**			
L210	Pleadings			$0
L220	Preliminary Injunction/Provisional Remedies			$0
L230	Court Mandated Conferences			$0
L240	Dispositive Motions			$0
L250	Other Written Motions/Submissions			$0
L260	Class Action Certification and Notice			$0
L300	**Discovery**			
L310	Written Discovery			$0
L320	Document Production			$0
L330	Depositions			$0
L340	Expert Discovery			$0
L350	Discovery Motions			$0
L390	Other Discovery			$0
L400	**Trial Preparation and Trial**			
L410	Fact Witnesses			$0
L420	Expert Witnesses			$0
L430	Written Motions and Submissions			$0
L440	Other Trial Preparation and Support			$0
L450	Trial and Hearing Attendance			$0
L460	Post-Trial Motions and Submissions			$0
L470	Enforcement			$0
	Total Hours and Fees	**0**		**$0**
	Litigation Costs			
1	Travel Costs (Assuming local venue)			
2	Deposition Costs			
3	Photocopy Costs			
4	Communication Costs			
5	Experts and Consultants			
6	Court Appointed Arbitrator/Mediator			
7	Graphics			
8	Other Costs			
	Total Costs			**$0**
	Total Fees & Costs			**$0**

In determining what tasks to budget, outside counsel heading the litigation effort should keep in mind Pareto's Principle: 80% of the results come from 20% of the causes. This is the 80/20 rule or the rule of the "vital few."[8] Put another way, once the team has gathered 80% of the available information (in the form of relevant documents, witness testimony, and expert opinions), the other 20% may not be worth the cost and time consumption involved in collecting, sorting, and analyzing it. In-house counsel should be closely consulted in the weighing of the costs and benefits of tasks that may fall within the category of things not worth doing.

A strategic case budget should be distinguished from a "burn rate" projection, which uses case staffing, projected percentage utilization of staff members during the applicable period, and costs associated with that mix of resources to estimate a monthly charge.

A strategic case budget also is not the same as a "usual cost" approach, which relies upon internal law firm experience with similar cases to make a projection of what a case or family of cases will cost.

The power of a thorough initial case assessment and strategic budget is the avoidance of unrealistic expectations and "sticker shock" on the part of the client. As the case develops, there inevitably will be discrepancies in the starting budget and actual costs incurred. The top reasons for budget discrepancies are scope change, team composition change, inefficient case management, communication issues within case teams, and overly optimistic initial assumptions about how the case will proceed. When discrepancies occur, communicate promptly with the client about them. In-house counsel and insurance underwriters are accountable for their litigation spend and must be equipped to explain changes in the budget. A good budget will set cost expectations and avoid surprises.

[C] Discussing Risk with Clients

An approach to the discussion of risks involved in a case is conceptually simple, but difficult to do well. Risk in complex litigation boils down to what we don't know. The method I've used with clients begins with an identification of possible pathways the litigation might take.

---

[8] Vilfredo Pareto was a 19th century Italian philosopher and economist who posited that 80% of the results come from 20% of the action. This principle flowed from his observation of unequal distributions of widely varying phenomenon such as land ownership in Italy and the production of peas from plants in his garden. We will return to this concept when we discuss the important reasons to avoid the "leave no stone unturned" approach to litigation in Chapter 4—Case Management.

"Here's how things could play out." Turn next to the probabilities and payoffs. "Here's what's likely (if possible, giving percentages), and what the costs and rewards are." Next, explain the transactional costs involved. "Here's what it's likely to cost to get there." Again, don't sugar coat it. Finally, cover possible organizational impacts. "Here's how long it will take, what will be required of your people, what the possible disclosure and regulatory consequences are, and what the potential reputational harms might be." The relative level of sophistication of the client will determine how you present this information, but these are the basic points that need to be covered.

A convenient device for synthesizing this information is the decision tree. Decision trees have been used in business for decades, but only gained traction in legal circles in the late 1970s and early 1980s. I first wrote about decision tree analysis in the mid-1970s in preparing a quantitative business analysis section for a marketing text.[9] The principles described then remain useful today although the practice has come of age with the advent of the computer and software that does the number crunching for lawyers, making this method even more user-friendly.

[D] Use of Decision Trees

Decision trees are a structured method of risk assessment that first puts uncertainties into perspective and then takes them into account in the decision-making process. Decision trees allow counsel to focus resources on pivotal issues and optimize actions that make a difference.

This quantitative method systematically examines variables in litigation that affect case value. Retained counsel anticipates the logical flow of the case in creating a diagram or decision tree of how the case might play out. Outcome probabilities are estimated for each branch of the diagram. Values of various potential outcomes are estimated. Then the probabilities of the outcomes multiplied by the values of the outcomes are summed to estimate an expected value for the decision tree.[10] This method then allows counsel to make probabilistic statements about

---

[9] *See, e.g.*, Burton Marcus et al., *Mathematics for Marketing—Decision Trees*, Modern Marketing 721 (1975).

[10] Decision trees follow a Sum of Product representation. The simplified formula for the calculation is: $E(x) = \sum_{1}^{N} x_1 p_1 ... x_n p_n$ where x = random variable with finite number of finite outcomes, p = probability of outcome, and E = expectation of x.

lawsuits that have meaning to clients, and to weigh the value of settlement versus trial. Litigation, after all, is about risk.

And risk is about uncertainty. If there is no uncertainty (probability of 0% or 100%) there is no risk. Risk has four components: (1) an event (*e.g.*, summary judgment); (2) the probability of the occurrence of the event (*e.g.*, a 25% chance the court will grant summary judgment); (3) the impact of the event (*e.g.*, if summary judgment granted, the case is over, and the plaintiff takes nothing); and, (4) on something of value (*e.g.*, judgment in favor of the client avoids the potential for a $100 million judgment).

Risk doesn't exist independently. It is not an entity waiting to be measured. It is an invention of the human mind to help us cope with dangers and uncertainties.[11] Classic risk management involves four tasks: (1) risk identification (issue spotting); (2) risk assessment (analysis and probability); (3) risk response planning (strategy development); and (4) risk response (strategy implementation). Litigation risk assessments by retained counsel typically focus on the first two, as response plans and execution of those plans typically occur within the business unit. For example, in toxic exposure cases resulting in personal and property injury, the litigators will be focused on the risks identified in the resulting lawsuits and the business unit will be focused on a plan to remediate the harm and avoid future releases.

There has been an evolution in litigation over the last several decades toward the use of decision-making tools like decision trees because the world is not a simple place, and complex litigation is an essentially complex phenomenon. Complex legal matters require multivariable risk analysis. This method requires a focus on both liability and damages issues and an understanding of the multiple potential scenarios that might unfold. Decision trees allow counsel to answer the question the client inevitably should and will ask: "What's the case really worth?"[12] And decision trees provide a short-hand outline of the pathways down which the litigation might travel. This, in turn, allows you

---

[11] Paul Slovic, Baruch Fischhoff, & Sarah Lichtenstein, *Response Mode, Framing and Information Processing Effects in Risk Assessment*, New Directions for Methodology of Social and Behavioral Science: Question Framing and Response Consistency 21–36 (Robin Hogarth ed. 1982).

[12] Focus group and mock jury research can provide case specific information about the likelihood of a particular result or case value. Services that report jury verdicts and settlements can provide more general information about the value of similar cases.

and the client to see how various events might influence case strategy and determine what actions might be worthwhile undertaking.

One additional use of decision trees in litigation is their role in settlement negotiations. Decision trees are useful, of course, in determining the value of a case—a necessary step in preparations for informal settlement discussions, mediations, or settlement conferences. In addition, a well-prepared decision tree can be used to explain how your client came to its position and to educate the mediator about the ways a case might develop. Sensitization of the decision tree with high, low, and expected outcomes in both the probability and the value of an outcome allows your client to demonstrate to the mediator the outer parameters of the expected value of a case. Output from a hypothetical contract case involving a suit between a coyote and a company called ACME might look like the following:

FIGURE 1-5

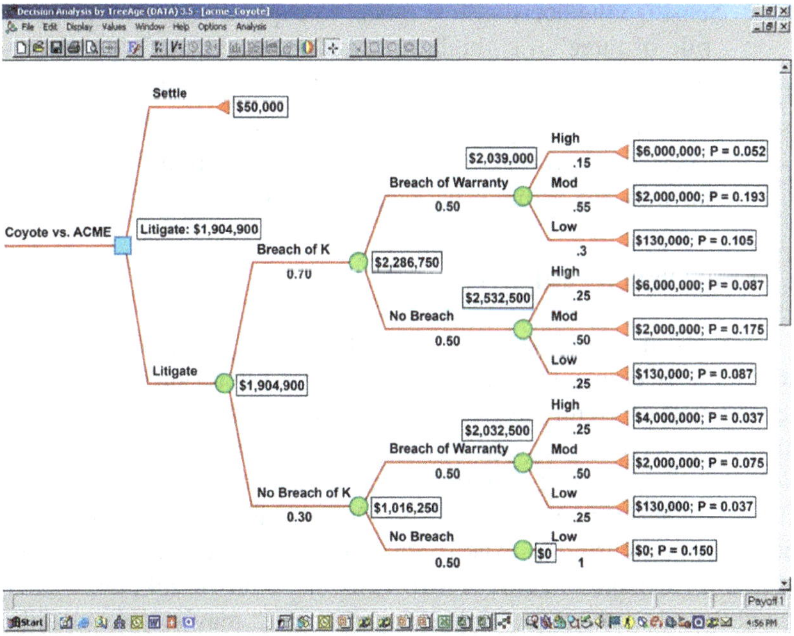

This decision tree uses Marc Victor's software.[13]

[13] Marc Victor, TreeAge Software. There are other software developers that offer decision tree programs. *See, e.g.*, DPL Decision Tree Software that links to Excel spreadsheets.

The preparation of decision trees has the benefit of bringing method to madness. This method encourages comprehensive discussion by identifying all likely outcomes determinative of the issues, consideration of the probabilities of individual events and their value, and analysis of realistic damage scenarios.

But decision trees are only as good as the inputs. Garbage in garbage out. What twists and turns will the case take? What are the odds of a particular event occurring? What is the value of that occurrence? Where do we get useful data to input into the analysis? Well, here are a few suggestions.

- Use mock jury and focus group research to set probabilities and outcome values.
- Use "marketplace" data (*e.g., Jury Verdict Alert*) for case values.
- Sensitize the decision tree model to explore ranges by using the "rule of three" (*i.e.,* high, low, and expected case) to make the client aware of the potential range of values of a case.
- Use plain old lawyer experience, also known as "horse trading experience," to make estimates of the probability of outcomes and what the value of the outcomes might be.

[E] Limits to Forecasting Accuracy

The client should be cautioned early and often that while detailed initial case assessments, strategic budgets, and decision trees provide large amounts of useful information to aid in decision making, they come with a risk. *They give the appearance of precision that is very difficult to achieve in litigation.* Litigation is an inherently complex process. Litigation plans change as facts are developed, witness testimony is taken (and sometimes changes), experts are retained and provide opinions, and court rulings shape the case. Further, as the "known unknowns" may become known or change, "unknown unknowns" may surface that alter our perceptions of the litigation.[14] These have ripple effects on the expected cost of the case, and the probable outcomes.

---

[14] Frank H. Knight, *Risk, Uncertainty and Profit* 197 *et seq*. (2006). Donald Rumsfeld channeled Prof. Knight in his famous statement: "There are known knowns—there are things we know we know. We also know there are known unknowns—that is to say, we

The economist and Nobel laureate Friedrich Hayek said of essentially complex phenomenon that the aspects of the events to be accounted for and about which we can get quantitative data are necessarily limited and may not include important ones.[15] So too with the phenomenon of complex litigation. Litigators simply can't know with precision the cost or outcome of a case, and can't know with certainty the path a case will take to resolution. We can only speak in terms of probabilities. And we can be wrong.

[F] Key Client Communication Opportunities

Periodic case reviews should be scheduled between client representatives and retained counsel to ensure the client is fully informed about the progress of the case and offered the opportunity to review case strategy and change it, if necessary.

FIGURE 1-6

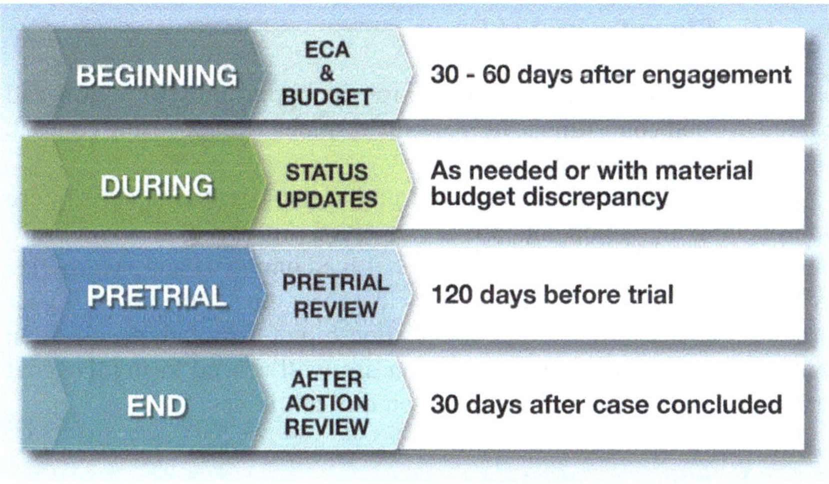

There are several natural points in the litigation that offer opportunities for detailed discussion:

- In the beginning when the initial case assessment and strategic budget are being prepared;

know there are some things we do not know. But there are also unknown unknowns, the ones we don't know we don't know."

[15] Bruce Caldwell, *Ten (Mostly) Hayekian Insights for Trying Economic Times* (2011).

- In status updates as needed or when material budget discrepancies are experienced;
- In the pretrial period, about 120 days before trial and when memorandum of contentions of fact and law and pretrial orders are being prepared, and
- After a judgment or verdict for an after-action review, about 30 days after case conclusion and as any appeals or post-trial motions are considered.

Additional informal reviews are appropriate as fact and expert discovery is about to conclude, but in time to schedule additional discovery, and in final trial preparation when key witnesses are readied for testimony. And in any event, additional reviews should be scheduled with the client when major developments occur in the case—good or bad. Examples might be a client financial crisis or intervention by regulators.

[1] Client Reviews of Drafts

Understand client expectations for the opportunity to review and comment upon court filings, key communications with opposing counsel, and other case-critical documents.

Start early, set deadlines, and nudge the client if deadlines are approaching and comments are not received. Provide a polished draft, but consider sharing advance outlines. Take comments and incorporate as appropriate, or propose alternatives that meet client objectives. If your firm has a lawyer with an ongoing relationship of trust with the client on matters other than the litigation, you are well served to involve that person in discussions with the client on difficult issues.

[2] Billing for Services

Another opportunity to communicate with your client regarding the status and progress of the matter is the monthly bill for your services. Lawyers tend to view their bills as a method of getting paid, and nothing more. But I suggest there is another purpose served by the preparation of billing statements that describe briefly but well what each member of the team did on each day of the engagement to move the proverbial ball down the field.

The days of the "For services rendered . . ." bill are long gone. The "death of the billable hour" has proven to be a false prophecy. Alternative fee arrangements have been easier to talk about than to institute. The current state of play, then, is a bill, usually rendered monthly, that provides information to the client about hours incurred by team members at an agreed rate leading to a total for services rendered together with a summary of all costs incurred on behalf of the client. This now-traditional approach to billing can be done well or poorly. It can result in additional information for the client about progress on their matter if done well, or great aggravation if done poorly.

The advice I always gave to my team members about the keeping of time notes and the rendition of bills was simple.

- Record your time on a client's matter as accurately as you can on a daily basis.
- Don't wait until the end of the billing period to prepare your time notes because you will sacrifice accuracy and forget what it is you did and how much time it took you.
- Write your time description in a way that tells the client what you did, why, and what work product was created by it. And write your descriptions so that someone reading the time entry will be motivated to pay you for that work.

The lawyer serving as the team leader (whether that was the lead trial lawyer or national coordinating counsel) would carefully review and edit the bill to make sure it was accurate. Time entries were checked to make sure they were on the proper bill and adequately described the work performed. Costs were reviewed to make sure unauthorized charges were removed from the bill. Finally, a cover letter for the bill was prepared giving a high-level summary of the activities the bill reflected, describing any discounts applied to the bill, and indicating any write-offs to services that were made.

My discussions with many in-house lawyers over the years have convinced me that the way in which their firms bill for services is the source of most of the major gripes they have with their firms. Here are some of the most frequently mentioned.

- "Timekeeper names appear on my bill, but I've never met them, don't know who they are, and don't know what role they have in the litigation." I'll talk about the importance of acquainting the client with the team in later chapters. The message from clients is clear; introduce your team to your client so they know who is working on their matter.

- "I'm getting billed for items I view as law firm overhead—things like secretarial overtime, after-hours meals, and clerical tasks. This is the firm's cost of doing business, not mine." Your hourly rates ought to incorporate costs of doing business so you don't find it necessary to add charges for overhead items.
- "I've been charged for learning my business when that is something the law firm should do off the clock. My law firms should invest in the relationship by understanding our business." Invest in your client by learning about their business and the challenges it faces.
- "Every year I get annual rate increases based on higher costs of doing business and step increases for lawyers on the team as they progress in their careers. This is a double whammy." Make the case to your client at rate-setting time that you are providing exceptional value in the work of each team member on the case. Inflation, higher costs for personnel, and promotions are less interesting to your client than an understanding why your rates are competitive and your team is providing excellent value.
- "I frequently am charged for training more junior lawyers—for example, an associate sitting in court observing senior lawyers argue motions. This should be a firm expense, not a charge to me." When you invest in your people through training and professional experiences, your firm directly benefits from the enhanced abilities they possess. The client already pays for their services, and shouldn't have to pay for their development.

These complaints can do damage to the relationship between the law firm and the client and impair the successful representation of the company if left unaddressed.

§ 1.06 THE BOTTOM LINE

- Remember it's not about the lawyer, it's about the client.
- Don't let the litigation tail wag the corporate dog.

- Listen and respond to clients concerns and suggestions.
- Communicate clearly both orally and in writing.
- Be open to both praise and critique, and encourage client feedback on your services.
- Include on your team a person who can play "devil's advocate."
- Be willing to learn and adapt.

CHAPTER 2

STORYTELLING: THE ART OF THE ADVOCATE

"Whoever tells the best story wins."

—Will Rogers

A critical skill necessary to succeed as a trial lawyer in any case, but particularly in complex cases, is the ability to create a narrative that puts the facts in the best possible light for the client. The all-important task of identifying a defining theme and story line for the case is the responsibility of the team leader, aided by input from the team members. The story is the cornerstone upon which the case will be built, and is a necessary starting point for the development of the plan the team will follow.[1]

How often have you heard these phrases? "Let me tell you a story." "What's the story here?" "That's quite a tale!" "She's sticking to her narrative." "He's spinning quite a yarn!" In different ways, they attest to the importance of storytelling in our communications with one another. And to the centrality of storytelling in the way we talk with one another.[2]

At every stage of litigation, and in cases large and small, the art of the advocate is crafting a good story and telling it effectively so that the listener prefers your client's story over that of your opponent. Virtually every argument you make in litigation can be reduced to a story. And you miss opportunities to persuade a judge and jury to accept your client's version of the facts when you fail to do so.[3] As the American novelist Richard Powers noted: "The best arguments in the world won't change a single person's point of view. The only thing that can do that is a good story."

---

[1] This chapter is adapted from an article published in the American Bar Association's Litigation Journal. Don G. Rushing, *Storytelling: The Art of the Advocate,* 49 ABA Litig. J. No. 3, 16 (Spring 2023). I use the terms "storytelling" and "narrative" interchangeably for the purpose of this discussion, though a modern sense of "narrative" suggests a focus on structures and trends that evoke an emotional response rather than a history of events.

[2] *See* Philip N. Meyer, *Storytelling for Lawyers* (2014).

[3] Gerry L. Spence, *Story Telling,* 72 ABA J. Lawyer's Magazine 63 (Apr. 1, 1986).

§ 2.01 WHY THE STORY IS CENTRAL TO PERSUASION

The story is the original form of human thought, as old as humankind. Throughout human history, stories transmitted history, culture, beliefs, and knowledge from generation to generation, beginning with those stories told around the primordial campfire. The story is a method of teaching, "let me tell you a story," and a means of inquiry, "what's the story here?" Myths, parables, and fables are all examples of the story form. We are engulfed daily in stories: Television, movies, books, sermons, and songs tell us stories that reveal important principles and teach moral lessons.

The power of the story lies in its connection to human heuristics—the mental shortcuts we use daily to cope with our environment. Particularly, the heuristics of representativeness, which refers to a mental shortcut used to estimate probabilities, and the heuristic of availability, which is a mental shortcut used to make decisions on emotional cues and familiar fact patterns, are appealed to when we tell a story.[4]

A story invites both emotional and intellectual engagement by the listener. Stories are human constructs comprised of a mixture of facts, emotions, and interests that make an impression on us.[5] We too often think of emotion and reason as separate from one another. But neuroscientists tell us that the human brain's limbic system (the seat of emotional response) and neocortical system (the seat of logical thought) are wired together in the anterior and posterior cingulate cortices so that they work together. These two areas of the brain are in constant communication.[6] When we tell a story, we speak to both the logical and emotional parts of the brain.

Moreover, fMRI images of the brain show that colorful analogies and metaphors that enliven the telling of a story reliably and consistently activate brain regions, suggesting that humans are wired to respond to stories. Analogies are particularly potent in aiding understanding. For

---

[4] Daniel Kahneman, *Thinking, Fast and Slow* (2011). More will be said about biases, fallacies, and heuristics in Chapter 5—Litigation Decision Making when we discuss the process of deciding in litigation and some of the mental traps we can fall prey to in decision making in complex cases.

[5] Robert J. Shiller, *Narrative Economics—How Stories Go Viral & Drive Major Economic Events* 65 (2019).

[6] Edmund T. Rolls, *The Cingulate Cortex and Limbic Systems for Emotion, Action, and Memory,* Brain Structure & Function 224 (2019); Peter M. Vishton, *Understanding the Secrets of Human Perception* (2011).

example, if I say human thought processing and memory are *like* computers in that your "cranial hard drive" has stored information that your brain, *like* an operating system, can analyze and use, the point becomes more salient.

Finally, we remember stories. A story is a narrative that recounts a sequence of events in a memorable way. Unlike the recitation of a series of facts and figures that might flow over and run past a listener—even an attentive, motivated one—a story imprints on the memory. A compelling narrative provides handles for the listener's short-term memory to grab and hold onto the information provided through the characters and plot line. We learn best from examples. The story form teaches by providing a tangible example, tapping into basic human thought patterns.

Imagine if we had to go through law school memorizing the rules of the cases without the stories. Long after our first year Torts class, many of us recall the facts of *Palsgraf v. Long Island Railroad*,[7] but few of us can recite Justice Cardozo's holding in the case. Imagine trying to understand math without example problems, simply working from theorems and rules. My Calculus and Analytical Geometry instructor made this point very directly one afternoon when I went in to see him for extra instruction. After hearing me complain I didn't understand a proof of a theorem, he bluntly told me, "You're not Isaac Newton, just work the problems!" We learn and remember best when we have concrete illustrations that embed and demonstrate the underlying principles to be taught. In fact, many of us skip over the explanation of principles until we're provided with a concrete example of how the principle works. I wish I understood this before showing up for extra instruction in my math class.

§ 2.02 ADVANTAGES OF THE STORY FORM

Using a story to present your client's case has important side benefits. Your case presentation is more effective and natural. Litigation, and particularly trials and arbitrations, are stressful enough without adding to the burden with a presentation method that might appeal to lawyers, but that "real people" might find foreign or artificial. When you tell a story, you simply visualize; you don't have to memorize. You largely free yourself from notes. You speak conversationally. You connect better with the listener. You become a more powerful communicator. Your job as an advocate becomes easier.

[7] 248 N.Y. 339 (1928).

Moreover, you create space for the listener to enter into the narrative and make it their own. As Henri J. W. Nouwen sagely observed in *The Living Reminder*: "One of the remarkable qualities of the story is that it creates space. We can dwell in a story, walk around, find our own place. The story confronts but does not oppress; the story inspires but does not manipulate. The story invites us to an encounter, a dialog, a mutual sharing."[8]

§ 2.03 THE ELEMENTS OF A GOOD STORY

In the context of litigation, and particularly of trials, there are five key elements of an effective story: (1) theme; (2) characters; (3) motives; (4) plot; and (5) conflict. Let's examine each of these.

[A] Theme

A theme is the principle at play in the story; the central idea around which the argument is built. What do we do with this story? How are we to react? The concept of a theme should not be confused with your theory of the case—the legal framework upon which the case rests, including causes of action and affirmative defenses.

The theme of a good story explores a timeless, universal idea. The theme should do the work of unifying the law and facts into a coherent whole. A case theme creates the lens through which the listener views and interprets your story. Nobel laureate and Pulitzer Prize winner John Steinbeck believed that there is only one story in the world, the story of mankind wrestling with its own desires and behaviors in a contest between good and evil.[9] But there are endless variations on Steinbeck's Manichean worldview that the advocate may choose from to frame her argument.

What does a case theme—as opposed to a case theory—sound like? In a commercial case involving the sale of a business and a suit for rescission, it could be a common saying that captures the argument you wish to make: "a deal's a deal," "a man's word is his bond," or "her handshake was her promise." Or perhaps a Biblical reference: "When Esau sold his birthright to Jacob for a bowl of pottage, God refused to release Esau from his promise. Likewise, you should refuse to undo Ethan's sale of

[8] Henri J. M. Nouwen, *The Living Reminder* (2009).
[9] John Steinbeck, *East of Eden* (1952).

his interest in the family sheep ranch to his brother Robert because he now feels he sold too cheaply."[10]

An important caution, however. The theme you choose must match the audience. *A good argument made to the wrong audience is a losing argument.* The listener must be prepared to accept your story as the "truth." And as Thomas Kuhn had it in *The Structure of Scientific Revolution*, "truth" is a function of the paradigm within which one works.[11] This is not to say that there are no objective "truths." If truth means correspondence with reality, then fidelity to the facts surely matters. But my point is a different one. The listeners' attitudes, values, beliefs, and life experiences form the worldview or paradigm thorough which they assess your story and determine what to them is "true" or not.

A statement may be true in one paradigm and may be false in another. As an example, in physics the proposition that time passes at a constant rate is widely accepted as "true" in our world of Newtonian mechanics, but would be open to dispute in Einstein's world of relativity where how fast time passes depends on how fast you're traveling. Or in the realm of geometry, the proposition that the shortest distance between two points is a straight line is "true" in Euclidian space, but in Lobachevskyian space the answer would be a curve. All this is to say that you must pay attention to the audience you anticipate will be hearing and responding to your story. Craft your story with your intended audience in mind.

[B] Characters

Stories have characters; the actors who do things, say things, and write things. The litigants and witnesses are the characters in your story. They make your story interesting. Who are they and why should we care? What do they do and how do they do it? How do we know what they did?

We want the listener (in a trial, the trier of fact) to care about our characters and identify with them. Humorist and master storyteller Garrison Keillor suggests that characters are best seen at dog level. We want the characters that are favorable to our story to pet the dog, feed the dog, smell good to the dog, and the characters that are unfavorable to be uninteresting to the dog, or better still to anger the dog. We want our characters to be immediately understandable, accessible, and

[10] Genesis 25: 29–34.

[11] Thomas S. Kuhn, *The Structure of Scientific Revolutions* (3rd ed. 1996).

credible. Part of the hard work of the advocate in preparing her case, of course, is to determine which characters can tell the story in a credible manner, and to prepare them to give effective testimony in a trial or arbitration. Close attention must be paid by the team leader to the selection of witnesses who can carry the story persuasively without bringing unwanted baggage with them.

[C] Motives

The characters in our story have reasons for their actions. Motives interest judges and jurors, and almost always matter. While events tell the "what" of a story, motives tell the "why." Motives provide context within which the event should be interpreted.[12] Motives tell us how we should feel about an action, an event, or a conversation. Even when your legal theory of the case doesn't contain a scienter, intent, or state of mind element, *motive still matters*. Why does this witness so vividly remember the exchange with the plaintiff and why is he willing to give testimony about it? What could the boss have been thinking when she decided to terminate the employee without cause? Why didn't the company grasp that its product could be used for an alternative, dangerous purpose? Your characters' motives should be woven into the description of their actions so that the listener fully understands what transpired.

We want judges and juries to accept our characters' motives. We want the characters in our client's story to be noble, if possible. If not noble, then appropriate and understandable under the circumstances. And if nothing else, at least the product of human frailty and therefore forgivable.

[D] Plot

The plot is the sequence of events and the interplay of the characters. In a trial, the plot integrates the legal theory of the case with evidence, including witness testimony, documents, and demonstratives. In every case, you will be working with some variation of the typical litigation story arc: "At first everything was just fine, then something bad happened, now we have to remedy it."

---

[12] Robert M. Pirsig, *Zen and the Art of Motorcycle Maintenance—An Inquiry into Values* 70–72 (2005).

The advocate is the architect of the plot line. The plot doesn't have to flow chronologically. It can begin wherever you like. It can start at the very beginning and work forward in time. "In the beginning when God created the heavens and the earth, the earth was a formless void and darkness covered the face of the deep. . . ." Genesis 1:1-2. (Now there's a plot line that really starts at the beginning!) Or it can start at the end and work backward. "And they all lived happily ever after," but lots of things happened before that. Or you can start somewhere in the middle, work in either direction, cast a spotlight on an event or interchange that is central to your theme, then move to the cause or the effect. The "Star Wars" movies all begin with the introductory line: "A long time ago in a galaxy far away. . . ." The audience is then immediately thrust into the heart of the action somewhere in the middle of the timeline. The variations for organizing your story's plot are as limitless as your creativity and imagination.

But I say this with one reservation; people tend to understand more easily events that are presented in a chronological sequence. Whatever approach to the presentation of a plot line you may choose as the team leader, be mindful you will need to integrate the events you describe into a coherent timeline for the trier of fact. Chronologies showing events along a timeline or entries on a calendar are particularly helpful in teaching the listener how things unfolded in your case.

As you consider your theme and how you wish to develop your story's plot line, you must be true to the observable facts and logical inferences from those facts. Effective trial lawyers know they must aim for fidelity to the facts in crafting their narrative. If they don't, the consequence is a loss of credibility and persuasiveness.

I confess to frequently watching and enjoying reruns of *Castle,* an American crime/mystery television show that aired from 2009 to 2016.[13] The show starred Nathan Fillion as Richard Castle, a crime novelist, and Stana Katic as Kate Beckett, a New York Police Department homicide detective. The premise of the series is that Richard Castle, a highly successful novelist, becomes bored with his success and teams with Detective Beckett to solve the case of a copycat killer who re-creates murder scenes from Castle's novels. They solve the first case together, and realize their partnership could be successful in solving other cases if they combine their talents; Castle's ability as a

[13] *Castle: Flowers for Your Grave* (ABC Television broadcast March 9, 2009) created by Andrew W. Marlowe.

writer to weave themes and story lines from facts, with Beckett's creativity and relentlessness as an investigator to uncover evidence. Castle becomes an integral, if unorthodox, member of the crime-fighting team and is even given access to crime scenes and wears a bullet-resistant vest with the label "Writer" on it instead of "NYPD." In a neat reversal of the usual gender roles, Beckett is the one entering dark rooms with gun drawn, ready to arrest the bad guy, while Castle follows behind her trying to avoid injury.

I mention this television series in connection with theme and story line construction to make what I think is a critical point. You may be quite facile at developing interesting, compelling themes but those *themes must be supported by the facts.* As you learn additional facts, you may need to adapt or completely change your theme to match the evidence. A common element of the plot line of the *Castle* episodes has Richard Castle spinning story lines about how and why a murder might have occurred crime-novel-style, only to have Kate Beckett or her colleagues produce new evidence showing his story line is inconsistent with the facts. In response, Castle does what we must do as trial lawyers; he develops a new theme and story line that fits the new facts. Adapt, adjust, and overcome. But do so with fidelity to the evidence.

[E] Conflict and Resolution

Conflict in a story involves a controversy and the resolution of that controversy. In most stories, conflict drives the plot and creates the drama. But in litigation, unlike a play or novel, the facts largely are given to you to work with. You don't get to make them up. In litigation, the controversy is defined by the pleadings. The resolution sought is victory for your client. *The resolution you desire must be supported by a claim for justice.*

Judges and juries want to right wrongs. They want to respond to a plea for justice. They want to find for the party who has been injured, or that has been hauled into court and improperly forced to defend himself. You must tell your audience the specific wrong to be righted. You must give the jury a moral basis founded in law for the action you wish them to take.[14]

[14] These points are suggested by several noted trial advocacy experts. *See, e.g.*, Gerry Spence, *Win Your Case* (2005); Keith Evans, *Common* Sense Rules of Advocacy for

Within the limits of the causes of action and defenses involved in the legal controversy, you may choose the point of clash for your argument. Your story may agree in substance with the facts presented by the opponent, but offer a legal reason why your client still prevails (*e.g.*, a limitations period has run, or an absolute immunity applies). Or your story may agree that the plaintiff was terminated, but argue that the employment was "at will" and could be terminated for any reason or no reason at all. Or that while there was an injury to the plaintiff, there were no compensable damages flowing from the injury. Again, as the advocate you are the architect of your plea for justice.

§ 2.04 WHEN TO USE THE STORY FORM

You should *use your case's story at every stage of the litigation.* Effective storytelling in a lawsuit doesn't just begin at trial or in an arbitration proceeding. The preparation of your story starts when the case first comes into the office and continues through appeal.

Begin by identifying applicable jury instructions that cover the causes of action and affirmative defenses that are pleaded. This is the legal framework on which your argument will be based. They are the bones on which the flesh of the story is hung.

Precondition your judge or arbitrator by laying out your themes in pleadings, initial appearances, and dispositive motions. Your judge is an important audience for your story, even if the case will be tried to a jury. Early case appearances, such as scheduling conferences, provide a good opportunity to begin to tell your client's story.

If your judge invites you to a case management conference to settle upon dates for the progress of the case, and you think your client should not be in her court, perhaps because of improper venue or a more convenient forum elsewhere, take the opportunity to tell her so. "Your honor, this is a case about a tragic mid-air collision over the Amazon jungle in Brazil, between a passenger jet owned and operated by a Brazilian airline and an executive jet made by a Brazilian airplane company. All the passengers and crew were Brazilian residents. Both planes were under the control of Brazilian air traffic control when the collision occurred. The accident is under investigation by the Brazilian equivalent of our NTSB, and the physical evidence remains in Brazil. This case should be tried

---

Lawyers (2004); Keith Evans, *The Golden Rules of Advocacy* 66 (1993); James W. McElhaney, *From Start to Finish*, Am. Bar Ass'n J. 52–53 (Oct. 2000).

in Brazil. The first activity in this case should be a hearing on *forum non conveniens* motion." Tell a story.

In discovery, gather the facts that buttress your story and blunt areas of attack on your intended themes. If the facts don't come in as expected during discovery, be prepared to modify your story as necessary to conform to the facts. You may even have to change your case theme entirely to be consistent with the evidence. You must be prepared to follow the facts where they lead, and to adapt, adjust, and overcome.

In *voir dire,* ask questions that will alert you to your audience's likely reaction to your story before they've heard the evidence and been instructed on the law. Listen for juror attitudes, values, and beliefs that are potential barriers to accepting your story. Here, you are listening to the potential jurors' stories for signs they may not be open to your client's story. Don't be afraid to ask the proverbial Bob Dylan "how does it feel?" questions that give you insight into both what a juror thinks and how strongly they feel about issues important to your case.

For cause or peremptory challenges may eliminate the most problematic jurors, but you are a fortunate trial lawyer indeed if the entire panel will be attuned to your story. Further modification of your story may be necessary to speak effectively to the views of the jurors left on your panel.

You will develop the facts to support your theme through witness examinations. Volumes have been written about the conduct of direct and cross-examination. But from a storytelling standpoint, make sure you have a good understanding of who you need to call and why to ensure that all points of your story are covered by witness testimony. When introducing documents, use foundation as an opportunity to tell the history of the document and why it is important to the case. Even pieces of paper have stories.

Opening statement and closing argument allow you to tell your client's story directly to the trier of fact. Opening is an extremely important stage of a trial or arbitration because it gives you the opportunity to announce your theme and begin your story. What will the evidence show, and how is it consistent with the outcome your client deserves? But when you stand up to deliver your opening, you don't have to use the well-worn approach of introducing yourself, thanking the jurors for their attention, telling them you're going to give them a "roadmap" of the evidence, and then repeating fact after fact that will be (you hope) proved at trial. Imagine that you're writing a novel and describing some aspect of the case that will grab the listeners' attention.

You might begin by taking the jurors to the scene of an accident. "In the very early morning hours of February 21st, about 2:15 am, Mr. Harold Smith was sitting in the cab of his Burlington Northern locomotive parked at a highway crossing. It was cold, dark, and very foggy. So foggy he could not see the control lights for the next section of track a couple of hundred yards in the distance. As he was waiting for a call from the train in front of him to tell him it was safe to move forward, he felt a shock wave shake the hoses on his locomotive. He thought perhaps a semi-tractor trailer truck had hit the train. So, he got down to investigate. He put on his coat, took his flashlight, climbed down from the locomotive, and walked through a ditch near the train and across a field. What he barely could see about 50 to 100 feet across the foggy, frozen field was the tail of an airplane lying shattered against a telephone pole. This case is about how that plane wound up in that field on that dark, foggy night." You don't have to be boring.

Closing is the last chance to weave the facts and law into a complete story that compels the trier of fact to right a wrong and provide justice to your client. How have you delivered on the narrative you provided in your opening and why does that require a specific result? Come back to the theme you announced earlier in the case. If you've planned your case well, you planned it with the end in mind. Bring the case full circle in your closing.

§ 2.05 HOW TO EVALUATE A STORY'S POWER

As you develop your client's story, frequently evaluate its power—its persuasiveness and salience—as you learn more about the facts of the case and the law that will be applied to it. I suggest you apply four tests to assess your story's power.

- ✔ Fit—Is your story true to the facts and does it preserve the appearances (*i.e.*, is it consistent with what we know to be true)? Does it do so honestly and without finagling?
- ✔ Fertility—Does your story generate a satisfying explanation for the case? Does it allow room for a listener's perceptions? Does it accommodate new data?
- ✔ Effectiveness—Does it engage the listener, and is it interesting? Does it break down in the face of counterargument? Does it set out a workable principle?

- ✔ Simplicity—Is it easily understood? Does it observe Ockham's Razor? (*i.e.*, the law of parsimony that holds that with competing explanations, the simpler one is to be preferred).[15]

An accurate assessment of the strength of your story depends on the quality of the information you rely upon to measure fit, fertility, effectiveness, and simplicity. While there is great variability of human response to storylines, there are ways of developing data to help you assess how most people react, and what characteristics identify the outliers. Advertisers and politicians, among other professions, have relied for some time on focus groups to measure the saliency of their message. Lawyers use similar methods. Focus groups and mock juries provide useful information about reactions to key issues in your case, the quantum of damages likely to be assessed, the persuasive power of themes, and the values, attitudes, and beliefs of potentially dangerous jurors. Even simple exercises, such as the presentation of summary cases for each side to a group of non-lawyer staff members will assist in deciding whether your story will resonate with the ultimate trier of fact.

§ 2.06 THE PERFORMANCE ART OF STORYTELLING

Once you've done the hard work of crafting a good story, your job as an advocate turns to telling it in a way that engages the listener. Not everyone is a natural storyteller, but there are basic skills you can learn that will enhance your effectiveness. When it comes to oral presentations to a judge or jury, there are three primary techniques you'll want to employ.

First, rely on *the visual dimension of advocacy;* the images that carry your story and help explain the points you're trying to make. An important aspect of good storytelling is the use of visuals in hearings and at trial. If "seeing is believing," then add credibility and interest to your story by showing photos, documents, and physical objects to the listener to demonstrate your points. Images are tangible; they can be seen and touched and thus become very real to a judge and jury.

For many years, the education and psychology literature has taught us that there are four primary styles of learning: visual, reading and

[15] These tests are a synthesis of approaches to the evaluation of arguments suggested by Professor Emeritus James T. Hall of the University of Richmond. *See, e.g.*, James T. Hall, *Practically Profound: Putting Philosophy to Work in Everyday Life* (2005).

writing, kinesthetic, and aural.[16] While this classification is controversial,[17] almost all of us have a predominant learning style, but rely on aspects of each style for our comprehension. Our learning styles or preferences form the way in which we receive information. These styles vary by sex, educational background, and other factors, and may change over time. The percentages of the U.S. population falling into these categories also vary in different studies depending on how the categories are defined. But there are some generalizations that can be drawn about learning styles and how to teach things to judges and jurors that are valuable for trial lawyers.

Those that learn best through reading and writing prefer to get their information in print. The paradigm is the library reading room. They thrive on documents and like to take notes. This is the primary path to judges—the written brief. Those that learn best this way comprise about a third of the population.[18] Show them the documents, blown up on poster board or displayed digitally on a screen. Show them the deposition or trial testimony. Let them see what others have written or said.

Those that learn best through visuals prefer to get their information from charts, graphs, diagrams, schematics, photos, videos, and so forth. The paradigm is the photo or chart. Those that learn best this way love the visual element—the diagram that shows them how something works, the map that tells them where something happened, or the timeline that lets them see how events played out chronologically. They comprise about two-thirds of the population.[19]

---

[16] Despite numerous studies of different learning styles, particularly the so called VARK categories (verbal, auditory, reading, and kinesthetic), there does not appear to be good evidence for the notion that matching activities to an individual's learning style improves learning. Harold Pashler, Douglas Rohrer, and Robert Bjork, *Learning Styles: Concepts and Evidence,* 9.3 Psychological Science in the Public Interest 103-119 (2008). However, there are ways of teaching particular subject matter that are better than others using the various learning styles. Matching the approach to the content can improve learning outcomes. *Id.* at 116.

[17] Paul A. Kirschner, *Stop Propagating the Learning Styles Myth*, 106 Comput. & Educ. 166–171 (2017).

[18] *See, e.g.*, William C. Bradford, *Reaching the Visual Learner: Teaching Property Through Art*, 11 The Law Teacher (2004) (available at SSRN: https://ssrn.com/abstract=587201 (Sept. 1, 2011)).

[19] Regine Zopf, Claire Marie Giabbiconi, Thomas Gruber, & Matthias M. Müller, *Attentional Modulation of the Human Somatosensory Evoked Potential in a Trial-by-trial Spatial Cueing and Sustained Spatial Attention Task Measured with High Density 128 channels EEG*, 20 Brain Research, Cognitive Brain Research 491–509 (2004).

Those that are kinesthetic learners prefer to receive their information by the hands-on experience, by touching and feeling. The paradigm is the shop or lab setting. Those that learn best this way appreciate seeing objects involved in some way in the case—the gun, the tire, the broken valve head, the bent airplane wing, or models of the scene. And they want to see you and your witness handle and, if permitted, pass around the object for inspection. They comprise about 5% of the population.[20]

With the vast majority of the population—including your judges and jurors—wanting to see or touch to believe, it comes as no surprise that one of your tasks as litigation team leader is to develop a good trial graphics and demonstratives program at the outset of the litigation. Find a good trial graphics and a trial technology person and include them as an integral part of the trial team. Get them started at the first stages of the litigation in helping to craft the themes and story that will guide case development. I was blessed as a trial lawyer to work closely over my career with a gifted trial technologist who had the visual creativity I lacked and was able to take narrative themes and put them into graphics that would help carry the story. We made a good team. This type of resource won't necessarily make your job easier, but it will improve your effectiveness as an advocate.

Good trial graphics, including document blow ups, deposition excerpts, photographs, diagrams, and demonstratives, can be used at various stages of litigation with powerful effect. Your argument at hearings that begin to tell your client's story can be enhanced with the use of graphics. Settlement conference presentations are made more salient and persuasive when you appeal to the visual aspects of learning. And, of course, the use of the visual element at trial will keep your judge and jury engaged and better able to follow the presentation of evidence and your argument for your client's position.

If the sequence of events is important to your story—and most times it is—create a compelling timeline of key events that lays out for the judge and jury in visual form what you explain to them verbally. For example, in a case involving the sequence of events leading to the crash of a privately owned airplane piloted by the owner and a professional pilot, a flight path reconstruction based on radar returns was created to show the aircraft's position over the ground and altitudes at specific

[20] Frank Coffield, David Moseley, Elaine Hall, & Kathryn Ecclestone, *Learning Styles and Pedagogy in Post-16 Learning—A Systematic and Critical Review,* London: Learning and Skills Research (2004).

times. The exhibit allowed jurors to visualize where things happened and when so that the story of the flight was more easily understood. This is what the exhibit looked like.

FIGURE 2-1

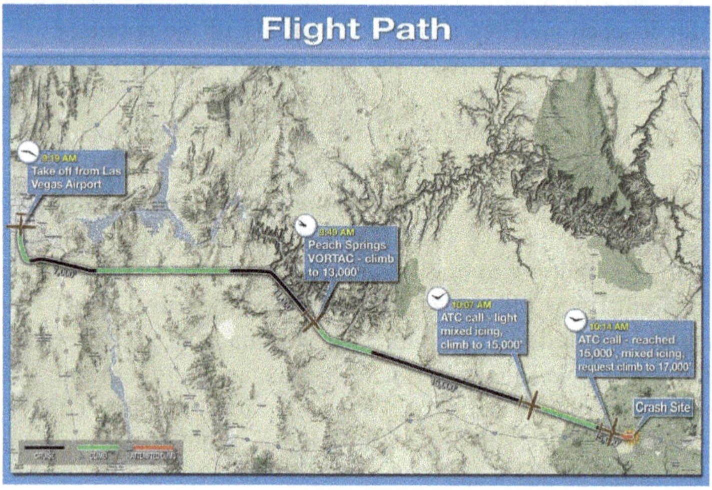

Second, *use your body to communicate non-verbally with your audience.* Stand erect with a comfortable posture. Keep your head up and make eye contact with the court and jury. This will give the impression of confidence and alertness, and make it easier for listeners to hear you.

You will want to be on your feet. Of course, you must comply with any limitations the court imposes on counsel that dictate where you must and must not stand when addressing the judge and jury. I have a vivid recollection of standing to make an argument during a hearing before a Texas federal court judge and being told in no uncertain terms: "Counsel for Defendant can sit down!" Yes, ma'am! Some jurisdictions have very strict rules, for example, about staying out of the "well" (*i.e.*, the area between the bench and counsel tables), remaining back from the jury box, and remaining in contact with the lectern, or even seated at counsel table. One of my co-counsel rested his hand briefly on the jury box rail while cross-examining a witness, and was promptly reprimanded by a judge who told him to "back off and stay away." Within those limitations, however, you'll want to position yourself so that you can see the jury and they can see and hear you. If possible, avoid standing behind a lectern or seated at counsel table as you tell your client's story. Lecterns and tables limit your gestures and movement and separate you from your intended audience.

Move for effect, particularly to signal a change of topic. Place physical evidence, copies of documents, and demonstratives (*e.g.*, blow ups of photos, documents, and deposition or trial testimony) around the courtroom so that you can move to them and show them to the jury or judge. Don't be afraid to handle the exhibits, particularly the "hot" ones. Holding a document in your hands while examining a witness or making an argument, even if the exhibit is displayed digitally before the judge or jury, sends the metamessage that it is important and you're not afraid of it. And use gestures to animate your storytelling.

Third, *use your voice—not just what you say but how you say it—to add interest to your story*. Be conscious of the pace of your speech. When we're excited or nervous, we tend to speak more rapidly, making it difficult for the listener to capture everything we're saying. Consciously slow down the rate of your speech unless you are deliberately using moments of rapid delivery to show excitement or passion. Repeat phrases for emphasis, and pause at important points to allow the listener to digest what you've just said.

Avoid a monotone delivery. Modulate your voice—high, low, fast, slow—to add interest and variety to your delivery. Speak loud enough to be heard, but please—no shouting at the judge or jury! Your objective is to use good projection and enunciation at a volume easily heard. When you wish to verbally underscore a point in your story, speaking softly is often the best way to draw in the listener.

Create rhythm and flow in your delivery to maintain interest and reinforce your story's message. The use of parallelism and repetition are rhetorical devices that aid in creating rhythm. I frequently would use a series of short leading questions in beginning direct examinations of experts, for example, to quickly introduce the witness to the jury. (Yes, you can lead on direct to develop a witness's testimony—particularly on preliminary matters not in dispute. *See* Fed. R. Evid. 611(c).) After the witness was sworn and stated his name, I would start with a short series of leading questions. "You are the Dean of the School of Engineering at the University of Washington?" "You are a member of the American Academy of Arts and Sciences?" "Your area of expertise is aircraft inflight icing?" "Please tell us why you're here today." If you heard strains of the opening bars of Beethoven's Fifth Symphony (da da da daah) in this example, you sensed the beginning rhythm of the examination.

Consider rehearsing your story in front of others to get comfortable with your presentation and efficient in your delivery. We can become so immersed in our case that we forget the listener does not have the same level of familiarity with the facts as we do. We might forget to define terms and provide background that is essential to the listener's understanding of the narrative. In very technical cases, I would fall prey to this pitfall and begin to use terms the testifying experts were throwing around without stopping for a definition and explanation. Keeping an eye on the trier of fact to catch any blank looks will help avoid this problem. Telling your story to lay people who know nothing about the case before you tell it to the trier of fact also will help you avoid this pitfall, and is a good way of assessing how jurors might react. I was always leery about leaving my best argument in the law firm conference room and losing spontaneity and energy from rehearsal, but what I learned in practicing the argument before an audience of lay people more than made up for it. And remember that brevity is a big virtue in advocacy. Practice helps you tighten and shorten your presentation.

There is another, frequently overlooked, reason why involving lay people in your practice sessions is beneficial. The secretaries, word processors, paralegals, and office staff members that provide invaluable support to the legal team can be your audience. They will enjoy being included in your preparation. You not only will learn from their comments, but will reward them for their help.

Use of these tools will make a significant difference in your effectiveness as a storyteller. If you use the story form at every stage of litigation, you'll live happily ever after.

Chapter 3

LEADING THE TEAM

"If your actions inspire others to dream more, learn more, do more and become more, you are a leader."

—John Quincy Adams

I learned whatever leadership skills I have in my time in the military at the U.S. Air Force Academy and as a junior officer in the Air Force, in an M.B.A. program at U.S.C.'s Graduate School of Business, and as a law firm leader serving as a Managing Partner of San Diego-based Gray, Cary, Ames & Frye, CEO and Co-Chair of Gray Cary Ware & Freidenrich, and Chair of Morrison Foerster's litigation group. I benefited from watching effective leaders in action along the way, and made it a practice throughout my career to read books and articles from the extensive literature about leadership. Each of these experiences gave me insights through various lenses into what it means to be a leader, and what leaders do.

I am deeply grateful for the leadership opportunities I've had at various points in my career and look forward to sharing with you some leadership lessons I've learned that may help you lead teams handling complex litigation. I've found that some of the leadership methods learned in other contexts—be it the military, the academic environment of an M.B.A. program, or the challenging setting of law firm management—can be applied effectively to the leadership of teams handling complex litigation.

Let's be honest, most lawyers aren't trained to be leaders and have no desire to be placed in positions of leadership. The standard law school curriculum doesn't contain formal leadership training. Few law schools offer courses in leadership development. Many lawyers go straight from their undergraduate education to law school without passing through the military or the business world where they might pick up some leadership skills. Lawyers tend to be very smart, capable, driven human beings who think and write well and are deeply committed to their profession. Some people happen to be natural leaders who like the responsibilities associated with leadership. But the personality types that often are attracted to the practice of law don't always lend themselves to either leading or following in a team environment.[1] Leadership skills can be learned, however, and are vital for those wishing to effectively lead teams in complex litigation.[2]

While I'll sometimes use litigation management as a term that encompasses team leadership and case management—and while they often overlap—they are not identical. And I don't think they require the exact same gifts. In my experience, leadership is concerned with effectiveness and doing the right things,[3] while management is concerned with efficiency and doing things right. Put another way, leadership is vision and inspiration,[4] and intentional influence toward a shared purpose; management is organization and administration of your team and its resources to function efficiently. Both are crucial to the success of a litigation team. We'll talk about leadership skills and methods in this chapter, mixing the theoretical with the practical, and management techniques in the next.

---

[1] Research using the Big Five theory of personality, now the predominant theory in personality research, found that traits in lawyers include neuroticism, competitiveness, aggression, introversion, perfectionism, cynicism, and a strong preference for thinking over feeling. Colin James, Miles Bore, & Susanna Zito, *Emotional Intelligence and Personality as Predictors of Psychological Well-being*, 30(4) J. Psychoeduc. Assess. 425–38 (2012).

[2] John Gardner, *On Leadership* 6 (1990); Leah W. Teague & Stephen L. Rispoli, *The Study of Leadership Theories: Great Leaders Are Made, Not Born*, American Bar Association Law Practice Magazine, November/December 2021.

[3] Peter F. Drucker, *Management: Tasks, Responsibilities, Practices* 44 (1974).

[4] Kim Campbell, *Flying in the Face of Fear: A Fighter Pilot's Lessons in Leading with Courage* 79 (Wiley 2023); Scott S. Barker, *Reflections on Trial Lawyer Leadership*, Colorado Lawyer, September 2023.

§ 3.01 LEADERSHIP MODELS

Since at least the time of Plato 2,400 years ago, philosophers have struggled with the complex phenomenon of leadership. The concept of leadership is very difficult to define, and changes as the context varies.[5] Several of Plato's most famous dialogs—*Republic, Gorgias, Statesman,* and *Laws*—offer insights into leadership traits, methods, and ethics.[6] Plato's dialogs speak mainly to characteristics of political leaders, both good and bad. But the leadership models he describes have potential application to modern leaders in settings other than politics.

Plato's leadership models highlight aspects of what a good leader does. These include the Doctor, the Navigator, the Artist, the Teacher, the Shepherd, the Weaver, and the Sower.[7] Scores of authors since the ancient Greek philosopher and wellspring of leadership thought have studied and written on the subject of leadership, frequently with close affinity to one of Plato's models.[8]

You will develop your own leadership style, but it may prove useful to understand Plato's models and variations on those models by modern leadership experts. The leadership characteristics outlined by the ancient Greek philosopher and important modern writers that seem to me most germane to the leadership of litigation teams are the Artist, the Navigator, the Weaver, and the Doctor. These roles have in common an

---

[5] Fred Fiedler & Martin Chemers, *Leadership and Effective Management* (1974).

[6] Dominic Scott & R. Edward Freeman, *Models of Leadership in Plato and Beyond* (2021) (provides an excellent summary of Plato's key dialogs on leadership and the leadership models the dialogs inspired). Perhaps the best that can be said is that the concept of leadership in a variety of contexts shares overlapping similarities, like Ludwig Wittgenstein's notion of "familial resemblance."

[7] Plato's models of leadership included the Doctor (who cares for others, works for the benefit of others, and exercises technical expertise), the Navigator (who executes a plan for the benefit of others, and does so expertly), the Artist (a visionary able to help others transcend the status quo with integrity); the Teacher (who moves others to change through appeals to rationality), the Shepherd (who is concerned only for the well-being and protection of others), the Weaver (who is able to blend together different types of people into a cooperative, unified whole), and the Sower (who originates ideas, spreads those ideas to others, then empowers others to act on them). *See* Scott & Freeman, *supra.*

[8] *See, e.g.*, James M. Burns, *Leadership* (1978) (on transformational leadership through the use of the Artist and Navigator models), James Collins, *Good to Great: Why Some Companies Make the Leap ... and Others Don't* (2001) (through use of the Weaver model); Robert K. Greenleaf, *Servant Leadership—A Journey into the Nature of Legitimate Power and Greatness* (1977) (through use of the Doctor and Teacher models).

emphasis on genuine caring for others and the possession and exercise of objectivity and expertise. Here's why I place particular emphasis on these four Platonic models of leadership as worthy of emulation by you as a litigation team leader.

[A] The Artist

A litigation team leader must have the ability and willingness to develop a vision for how the litigation should unfold. The Artist places issues in context and creates plans to overcome problems that to others might seem insurmountable. The Artist exercises creativity as well as detachment, the ability to stand a bit above the fray to see the big picture and to envision a way forward.

[B] The Navigator

Once the leader has convinced the team of the soundness of a vision for the litigation—the destination or objective to be attained—the leader must create a plan to accomplish that vision. The Navigator skillfully steers the team toward their shared goals. The Navigator isn't afraid to "stand apart from the crowd."[9] The Navigator is someone who gives the team a sense of common purpose and direction and motivates the team members to support each other toward the achievement of that common purpose.

[C] The Weaver

As the leader finds members to staff the team, he weaves people together into a cooperative whole. Part of the Weaver's job is to not only find strands to weave into a completed cloth, but to identify and discard strands that don't fit. A good leader weaves the virtues of both courage and moderation into his own character and reflects those virtues to other team members.[10]

---

[9] Scott & Freeman, *supra* at 47.
[10] *Id.* at 117.

[D] The Doctor

Doctors and lawyers share the concept of service in the interests of others. Doctors tend to the needs of their patients, lawyers to their clients. And we expect a high level of professional expertise from the practitioners in each profession. The Doctor promotes the well-being of the client. And in the context of complex litigation, the Doctor is objective, imposes order, solves problems, and effectively persuades people to accept the plan for the litigation.

[E] Concepts of Leadership

I've tried to distill the key concepts of leadership in the context of complex litigation to a few simple, but hopefully useful definitions. Leadership is the art of encouraging, influencing, and directing your litigation team to accomplish a mission. Leadership is about setting a vision, inspiring others to accomplish it, and empowering the team to take the necessary steps to achieve a goal. Leadership is about creating a culture of integrity, teamwork, and excellence.[11]

I also have arrived at a few simple statements about what leaders do and don't do. Leaders build the human chemistry vital to a highly functioning team. A leader's job is to transmit vision into action through the efforts of their team. The leader guides, cares for, and supports the litigation team in the accomplishment of the mission defined by the client. The leader is *not* self-involved. It isn't about her, it's about the client and the team.

As the head of a litigation team, I always strived to be the leader whose contagious enthusiasm and optimism motivated my team. (I consider myself a "realistic optimist.") I found that no one is motivated

[11] The core values of the U.S. Air Force Academy are: "Integrity First, Service Above Self, Excellence in Everything We Do." These three values are displayed on the wall above the ramp from the terrazzo to the parade ground at the Academy. When I was a Cadet at the Air Force Academy, the inscription on the wall read "BRING ME MEN." These words are from the first line of a poem by Sam Walter Foss that says: "Bring me men to match my mountains." At the time, this was an apt, inspirational statement for Cadets at an all-male service academy set at the base of Colorado's Rampart Range. But once women were admitted, a new message of inspiration was required. Under the leadership of Air Force Chief of Staff General Ronald Fogelman, the Air Force adopted the three core values of integrity, service, and excellence, and those words replaced the words of the Foss poem.

by an uncertain trumpet. No one thrives amid confusion and lack of direction.[12] I aimed to keep a steady hand on the tiller.

Many years ago, a team of lawyers from my firm parachuted into a very large, complex environmental contamination case at the request of a group of insurance underwriters who were on the risk. The insurers hoped we could assist an existing group of defense lawyers as the case proceeded to a trial only four months away. The leadership of the client's existing team was divided between two lawyers with different areas of expertise and different ideas about how the case should be handled at the pre-trial and trial stages. As we quickly learned more about the case and understood the dynamics within the existing defense team, it became apparent that our role would be to drive the back of the proverbial hook and ladder fire truck.

To keep up morale among our firm's lawyers in the frenetic pace and hard work of the run-up to trial, I asked members of the team to take specific roles corresponding to issues in the case. These roles continued through trial with the briefing and arguing of motions and the presentation of witnesses. Ownership of a part of the problem gave our lawyers a greater sense of control and purpose. I also asked our team members to closely coordinate with existing defense counsel to make sure we were not squandering precious time duplicating effort. A shared task list helped reduce uncertainty about who was to accomplish the work. We began to work together with the existing team, and formed some good friendships along the way. We encountered many rough patches during the case, but we made it through a two-month federal court jury trial having aided the client and insurers in a difficult situation with our senses of humor intact. Efforts to keep confusion to a minimum and provide clear direction not only helped get us to the finish line, but aided team morale.

Let's turn to the key leadership attributes and behaviors that I think you will find allow your team to succeed in accomplishing your client's objectives. There are many ways of describing the characteristics and methods of effective leaders. No doubt the importance of these varies with the challenges the leader confronts. Your challenge is that of a trial lawyer directing a group of lawyers and their support team litigating an important case on behalf of a client. I offer five key characteristics I believe are vital to effective leadership of litigation teams.

---

[12] Telephone interview with Lt. Gen. (Ret.) Tome H. Walters (Sept. 14, 2023).

§ 3.02 INTEGRITY

Litigation teams need to trust their leaders. Warren Bennis noted: "Trust is the lubrication that makes it possible for organizations to work." Trust leads to high performance. Trust comes from shared objectives, shared commitment, and personal relationships that build connections among team members.[13] A leader develops trust from the team through unbending integrity—speaking the truth, doing the right thing, respecting others.

[A] Speak the Truth

Team members need to know that you will speak the truth to them, whether they are a client or a litigator working on the case. Truthfulness in all communications and actions—whether in large matters or small—is vital. Truth in this context doesn't mean the "my truth" locution that has become popular, but rather an absolute value of correspondence with reality and with observable facts.[14]

Of course, speaking the truth and operating upon it is tempered by the understanding there are possible alternative perspectives on what the facts are and how to interpret them. Alternative views should be seriously considered, if raised, even if you decide to respectfully reject them. When you do so, you'll find it very helpful to your team member to give reasons for your decision. This helps the team to understand your thinking and intentions.

During a federal court trial in a transferor court following a lengthy Multi-District Litigation proceeding, our trial team was faced with an important decision about whether to call a corporate representative who made an excellent witness to testify as the case neared the close of evidence. The court had given each side a time budget to adhere to, and though we were within our allotted time, we had other witnesses we could call that might make better use of our remaining time.

I gathered our trial team, assistant general counsel for the client, the client representative who was the potential witness, the representative of the underwriters, and lawyers for co-defendants around a conference table to discuss our strategy. I asked everyone for their perspective.

---

[13] Jordan Lewis, *Trusted Partners* 3-18 (1999).

[14] Albert Einstein said: "Anyone who doesn't take truth seriously in small matters cannot be trusted in large ones either."

Different lawyers and our trial consultant had varying views on the issue. There was not unanimity of opinion, but there was good thinking about the different options. Perhaps the best comment came from a wise in-house counsel who asked: "Do we really want to go back to talking about the company and the product when we want to focus on how the accident happened and why it doesn't have anything to do with the product?" After further discussion, I told the client representative he would have made a great witness for the company, but we would not need him to testify, and explained why using the rationale provided by in-house counsel. We spent the rest of the time together deciding how to use the time with other witnesses we would have spent with the company representative.

[B] Promote Professional Conduct

Your team needs to know that rules of ethics and professional conduct will be followed scrupulously, and you will never ask them to do something that is unethical or unprofessional. Each team member must know that no case is worth the compromise of your or their personal integrity.

Your team also should be confident that you will not lead through intimidation and fear. We've all known senior lawyers who were "screamers"—leaders who raised their voices, spoke harshly, and directed subordinates in disrespectful ways. This is not the behavior you should engage in or model to your team because it is unproductive of team cohesion and performance. This behavior destroys morale.

The leader models conduct by what she says and does. A leader's words and actions exemplify the standard to be met by every team member. The mantel of team leader necessarily means that you take responsibility for the performance of the entire team. No throwing team members under the bus. No passing the buck. This can be very uncomfortable for the team leader at times.

In an international arbitration where the tribunal had ordered the pre-arbitration production of almost a million pages of documents, we discovered midway through the proceedings that a few files a witness had relied upon, and the opponents viewed as important, inadvertently had been omitted from the document exchange. We promptly notified the tribunal of the omission, provided the documents, and offered to either rearrange the order of witnesses or briefly recess the proceedings to provide time for the opposition to review the material with one of their experts.

The tribunal was unperturbed by the disclosure. The opponents expressed outrage at the oversight, but did not wish a recess or a change in the order of witnesses. The client, however, was unhappy with the error. The associate who was responsible for the document production was mortified at the mistake. I told the client I was responsible for the failure to produce the files, without identifying those who worked on the document production, and offered no excuses or explanation even though that would have been the easy path. I told the associate that mistakes happen, they are learning opportunities, and she should put the incident behind her and move on.

The incident turned out to be a tempest in a teapot, but the associate deeply appreciated the loyalty shown to her in an embarrassing situation. And she did learn from it. I also learned from the experience. On these occasions, you need to look in the mirror and ask yourself how you contributed to the problem. Was it the way you organized the effort, directed the task, or followed up to make sure all was done correctly? If you make a dog's dinner, you should be the first to sample the fare.

§ 3.03 COURAGE

One of the lessons I learned at the Air Force Academy is that the leader is the tip of the spear who leads from the front and does so with courage. The courage I'm talking about in the context of complex litigation is not the same as a soldier, sailor, or airman in combat who is courageous, willing to overcome fear and put life and limb on the line for country. But in the sense of a leader of an organization who holds herself and her teammates accountable, who is willing to have hard conversations with clients, team members, opposing counsel, and courts, who makes decisions crisply and confidently in ambiguous situations without perfect information, and who demonstrates grit, fortitude, perseverance, and aggressiveness. Courageous leaders perform well in the face of chaotic situations; they remain calm, slow down, take a deep breath, and plot a path forward that will address the problem.[15]

---

[15] Angela Duckworth, *Grit: The Power of Passion and Perseverance* 245 (2016); Campbell, *supra*.

[A] Responsibility

The team leader is the one who takes on the hard jobs, arguing the key motions, dealing with the client when things aren't going well, taking the key depositions, leading the team at trial, *or* assigning those jobs to those that are in the best position for the client to do the job. The "or" is an important one in this context. Delegation is not a dirty word. Too often, the team leader decides to argue a motion another lawyer briefed and understands better. On occasion, the lead trial lawyer decides to argue an appeal when accomplished appellate lawyers are more capable of handling the argument. Likewise, the team leader may be best positioned to explain an issue to the client, negotiate with opposing counsel, or take a key deposition because the leader believes he can be more effective, even if another team member has done the pick and shovel work to prepare to accomplish the task.

This is a judgment call that initially should involve team members who have done the work on the task and have detailed knowledge about it. What work already has gone into the task that will need to be repeated if the team leader takes responsibility for the task? How capable is another team member of doing the task if the team leader delegates the job to her? How confident are you that the client will accept delegating the job to another team member? On important issues, this is a decision that *must* be made with input from the client. But whenever the team leader decides to delegate a task to another team member, she should remember that the ultimate responsibility for the task will remain with her even though the authority to act has been transferred to another.

I observed how delegation of tasks can be done effectively from one of my mentors who had a trial conflict and needed to lateral a case to me. This senior lawyer and I called the client together. He explained that he could only be in one place at a time, and that a federal judge had told him exactly where he would be at a particular date and time. This would prevent him from trying the client's state court case set for the same trial date. He expressed the conviction that a continuance of the client's matter to accommodate my partner's trial schedule was not in the client's interests. He then asked the client "do you trust me?" The client assured him that he did. My partner then introduced me, told the client that he held the client and the client's interests close to his heart, and in turn trusted me to take the matter to trial and win. He asked permission to have me take over the case. The client asked a few questions about how that would work and who would bear the costs of me coming up to speed in the case. After receiving assurances, he agreed. I always felt it was a mark of true courage on the part of my partner to acknowledge the bind he was in and offer the client a solution that seemed to meet everyone's needs. A few months later as the case proceeded to trial, we reached a favorable settlement.

Sometimes, I've been on the delegating end of the situation. A younger partner and I were to co-try a commercial dispute over commissions on the sale of a consumer product manufactured by a foreign corporation. My partner had done an excellent job of preparing the case for trial, had worked very closely with the client to develop the case, enjoyed the client's trust, and had the courtroom experience necessary to successfully take the case to verdict. I thought he would do an excellent job first chairing the trial. The client knew who I thought should take the lead at trial and concurred. When we reported for the pre-trial conference, the federal judge who would try the case looked at each side and asked who the lead trial lawyer would be. After a brief silence at our table, my partner looked at me waiting for me to respond. I nodded at him and he, in turn, rose and told the judge he would be the lead trial lawyer. My partner did an excellent job for the client sitting in the first chair. I felt comfortable sitting in the second chair. And he never once asked me to carry his briefcase.

[B] Professional Growth

Giving others an opportunity to handle motions, discovery, and communications with clients has secondary benefits. Not only does it place the most knowledgeable, effective team member in a position to act, but it also allows team members to grow professionally and gain confidence. And giving such opportunities to others works wonders for team morale. When a leader entrusts someone with responsibility, it shows them that the leader is willing to invest in them professionally. It says they are trusted, valued team members. Trusting a task to someone else involves risk, but courageous litigation team leaders accept those risks for the good of the client and the team.

§ 3.04 VISION

When it comes to complex litigation leadership, the essence of vision is a plan to win.[16] The *Alice in Wonderland* "if you don't know

---

[16] The oft quoted line from Sun Tzu's *The Art of War* is that: "Victorious warriors win first and then go to war, while defeated warriors go to war first and then seek to win."

where you are going, any road will get you there" approach to litigation is not a formula for success.[17] Effective litigation doesn't come from simply doing everything the rules permit. It comes from planful action that makes use of the rules to accomplish a specific objective.

[A] Roadmap to Victory

A good litigation team leader will develop what Judge William Alsup referred to as a "roadmap to victory." The "roadmap to victory" is a powerful tool for alignment of client and counsel. It is a method for setting priorities and defining the critical path. This roadmap should be developed with input from the entire team, but the leader must own the plan.

I've found that the inclusion of key team members in brainstorming sessions as you put together the initial case assessment and develop case themes is a helpful way of assembling that all-important "roadmap to victory." Of course, including the client representative to provide client perspective is a necessary way to gain early alignment on client and team objectives.

[B] Communication

Once you've outlined your roadmap to a successful result, you'll want to share your vision with your client and litigation team. Let them know what the mission is, what the plan is for accomplishing that mission, and how the team members fit into that plan.

Communicate as many of the details of the plan as you're able to share with the team. I frequently would acknowledge uncertainty about how things might play out, but would make sure everyone understood what the client's objectives and expectations were, how I proposed to get the team to that goal, and what my expectations were for each

Samuel B. Griffith, *Sun Tzu—The Art of War* (1963). Who knows what Sun Tzu really meant? But our modern understanding of his admonition is that those who find success in conflict enter the fray with a plan to win.

[17] This is a paraphrase from a conversation between Alice and the Cheshire Cat in Lewis Carroll's *Alice's Adventures in Wonderland*. The West Texas version says: "If you don't know where you are going, when you get there, you'll be somewhere else."

member of the team. I explained my strategic intent;[18] the reasons behind each goal and the process to be followed in accomplishing that goal. If your team understands your strategy, they will know better what to do, do it better, and require less detailed supervision. Encourage members to ask questions so they have clarity, then let the team perform.

Communicate, communicate, then communicate some more. But communicate efficiently; don't unnecessarily occupy the time of your team members with meetings, or be perceived as doing so. Keep your team focused on your vision to achieve victory for the client. Keep your team on the same page.

[C] Look Down Board

A useful technique is to plan the case backward from the finish. As Stephen Covey counsels, "start with the end in mind."[19] Imagine what you will say in closing argument and how you want the court to instruct the jury on the law. Then plan as many of the steps as you can that will take you to that point. This involves as long a look down the litigation path as you can muster to anticipate the turns and potholes and find ways to steer around them. Ask what can go wrong and what will we do about it. Ask what the opponent can and is likely to do to derail your plan, and plan countermeasures that can be taken. Though you cannot foresee or control every eventuality as the case proceeds, planning backwards can go a long way towards minimizing surprises and setting you up to make the closing argument you envision.

This process worked well in one of the complex cases I litigated as team leader. After a tragic mid-air collision between two aircraft, a fully loaded commercial jet and an executive jet, on an international airway, suits were brought in multiple U.S. jurisdictions. My firm was retained to represent the designer and manufacturer of key components on board both aircraft. I prepared an initial case assessment of the type we discussed in Chapter 1, and engaged in detailed conversations with the client and its insurer to make sure we all shared the same vision for how the

---

[18] Gary Hamel & C.K. Prahalad, *Strategic Intent*, Harvard Business Review (July–August 2005).

[19] Stephen R. Covey, *The 7 Habits of Highly Effective People* 95–144 (1989); Campbell, *supra* at 62.

litigation would unfold. The case plan began with procedural steps to consolidate all cases in the federal courts in front of a single Multi-District Litigation judge and a *forum non conveniens* motion to dismiss cases filed in the U.S. court system in favor of a foreign jurisdiction, and ended with a general plan for how allocation of liability among potential defendants would be either mediated or arbitrated to a conclusion. The steps in the plan became milestones we were able, in most instances, to achieve. The case assessment—a vision for how the litigation would unfold—reassured the client and insurer that the litigation was being handled in a planful way, and allowed the team members to perform their roles with the bigger picture in mind.

But cases don't always proceed in the way you imagined them. A good leader knows and acts upon the old Yogi Berra line: "When you come to a fork in the road, take it." In complex, long-duration litigation, it often happens that you learn new facts, receive court rulings, or gain a new appreciation for what you thought you knew that forces you to rethink your approach. The path you marked out months or years ago may no longer be the best path forward for the client, whether best means "safest and most conservative" or "likely to enable a home run." Time to take the fork leading in a new direction.

To do so, you might look for "silver bullet"[20] solutions that shortcut or simplify the litigation. Creativity in action. Is there a better forum for your case? Is there a dispositive motion that will reduce the scope of the litigation, or even end it? Is there any procedural or substantive deal that can be negotiated to do either? What bargaining tools do you have and when can they best be used?

[D] Practice Humility

Your vision for the case should be tempered with a large dose of humility about what you think you know and what you think you don't know, while also appreciating that there always are unknown unknowns lurking out there.[21] We aren't as smart as we think we are, and it is good to be cautious about what we think we know.

---

[20] The term "silver bullet" is a metaphor for a simple, seemingly magical, solution to a difficult problem. In the late 1940s and 1950s television series "The Lone Ranger," the hero would always leave behind a silver bullet when the episode's conflict had been resolved successfully.

[21] *See* McKnight, *supra* at 198–210.

Complex litigation involves decision making under conditions of uncertainty. And the uncertainties frequently are many. What claims or defenses are legally sustainable? What will the evidence show, and what will be admissible at trial? What will the judge's attitude be toward your case, and how will she rule on important legal and evidentiary motions? What will your opponent's view of their case be, and how amenable will the opponent be to a resolution acceptable to your client? What will your jury panel look like, and how open to your theme and story line will they be?

In large, complex cases, I always relied on jury research of one form or another to gain an understanding of what a jury might think about my case, my themes, and some of my witnesses. I mock tried more cases than I tried to a judge or jury. A mock jury or focus group exercise helps to focus your attention not only on your own case, but your opponent's case as well. I think John Stuart Mill was right: "He who knows only his own side of the case, knows little of that."[22] The result of a well-conducted exercise also provides you with data to use in the preparation of the type of risk assessments we discussed in Chapter 1.[23] And it also aids in developing a profile of the characteristics of potentially favorable and unfavorable jurors. I've found that you should do whatever you reasonably can to reduce, or at least quantify, the uncertainties in your case and inform your case plan. Focused jury research can be a significant aid in doing so.

[E] Be Nimble

And yet be prepared to change plans. As General Colin Powell observed: "No battle plan survives contact with the enemy." You only control, at best, half of the litigation. You have opponents on the other side who are thinking of ways to derail your plan and block your "roadmap to victory." You may on rare occasion have a prejudiced, incompetent, or inexperienced judge. After the jury has been seated, you may find you have a panel that begins with a predisposition against you or your client. You will need to adapt, adjust, and overcome to win.

---

[22] John Stuart Mill, *On Liberty & Utilitarianism* (1993) (originally published in 1859).

[23] As mentioned in Chapter 1, jury research can provide information about the range of awards that might come from a trial and the probability of success at trial.

As the team leader, you should be open to changing course. We should continually evaluate why we do things, and consider how we might do things differently to do them better.

You will make mistakes and miscalculations. Instead of getting trapped in ruminations about mistakes you've made, it is far more important to analyze the root cause of the mistake as objectively as you can and learn from it. Then move on.[24] You won't forget the mistake—we don't have the ability to summon retrospective amnesia. But you can forgive yourself the error, understand the source of the failure, vow to do better next time, and move forward.

§ 3.05 TEAM BUILDING

Many years ago, I was asked by in house counsel for a Fortune 500 company to lead a task force to prepare a white paper on how to build collaborative work teams among in-house counsel and lawyers, accountants, analysts, trial technologists, and document management specialists from different organizations to serve the company in major pieces of litigation. This visionary lawyer and corporate leader asked that our task force design a "road map" for building effective collaboration among the team members. The effort turned into a very interesting study in cultural anthropology. We found we were describing in a litigation context how to build a "tribe."[25]

In my experience, team building involves, among other things, instilling in the team members the belief they are part of an organization defined by the three pillars of integrity always, service above self, and excellence in everything we do. In building a team, you are creating a culture of shared attitudes, values, and beliefs that will unite the members in a common effort. Here's the "roadmap" we came up with for the client.

---

[24] Campbell *supra* at 30, 116.

[25] The DuPont Primary Law Firm Collaboration Task Force published a paper describing the work of the group. Don G. Rushing, James D. Shomper, Deborah D. Kuchler, & Christopher Barbee, *Building the Virtual Law Firm Through Collaborative Work Teams*, ACCA Docket (Oct. 2001). Concepts and images from that article are borrowed for this book.

FIGURE 3-1

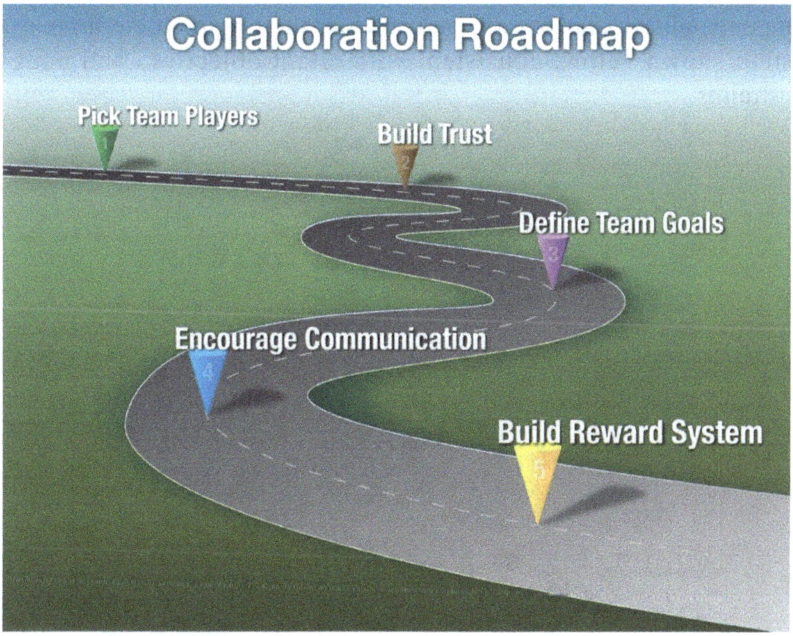

[A] Pick Team Players

The first step in building strong teams, either within your own firm or among law firms, starts with picking team players. These are people who can control their territorial instincts and "play well with others." No sharp elbows. You want good tool users—those that can adopt and use technology. You want good communicators—those that are effective in sharing information, not holding it close to acquire power. You want smart risk takers—people who are willing to intelligently assess and take risks and who will share the rewards and penalties of those decisions with the team. You want lawyers who are aggressive—on the balls of their feet and moving forward. You want trustworthy team members—those who are honest, loyal, reliable, and open. And you want people that are "givers" rather than "takers"; those that add to the mix of personalities and talents in a positive way and make those around them better.

You also should strive to populate your team with people possessed of the skill sets that will maximize the collective capability of the group. In litigation, this means recruiting to your team people who possess the substantive law, technical, and context expertise necessary to meet your client's needs. Your objective is to find resources to move the aggregate team capability as far out as you can from the origin on the three-axis system shown below, consistent with client objectives and budget constraints.

FIGURE 3-2

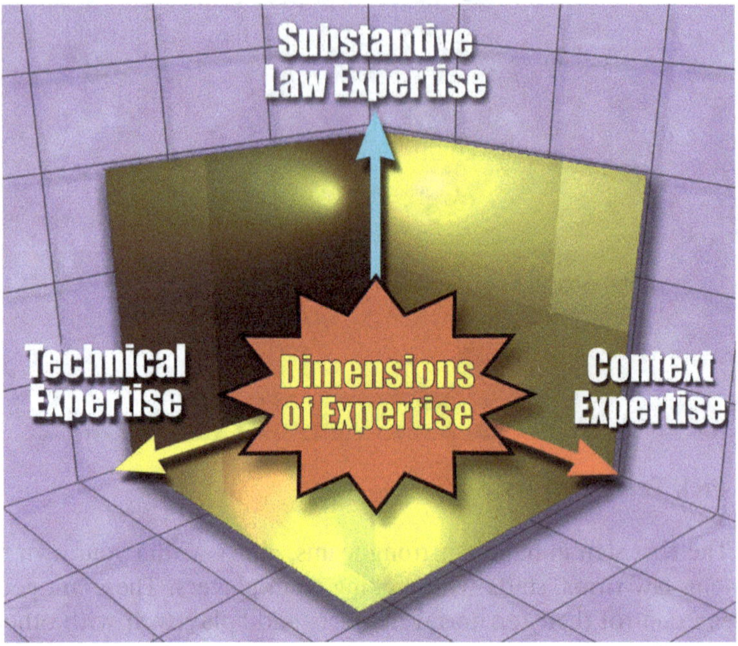

Each team needs a lead trial lawyer—someone with deep courtroom experience who can confidently try the case. If that isn't you (yet) find someone who fits the description. If you are litigating the cases in several different jurisdictions, a national coordinating counsel responsible for keeping everyone on the same sheet of music is vital. The lead trial lawyer and national coordinating counsel don't have to be the same person, but frequently are.

Bring to the team lawyers who are accomplished in the substantive area of the law. If it is an antitrust case, for example, find someone with a strong grounding in that area of the law. Find someone who has litigated the type of case your client is confronted with. If the case arises out of an aircraft crash in another country, your team should include someone who has traveled the road of international aviation accident litigation. If the case involves the release of toxic substances into the environment, find an environmental lawyer who understands the federal and state regulations bearing on the release and the duties of the potentially responsible persons. The point is straight forward; complex litigation is not an opportunity to learn a new area of law on the job.

Even very bright, accomplished lawyers are at a disadvantage when practicing out of their field in complex litigation. I observed an outstanding Washington, D.C. white collar crime law firm with first rate trial lawyers struggle in a series of aviation product liability cases because they did not have familiarity with applicable Federal Aviation Administration regulations concerning certification of aircraft, rules pilots must follow in operating aircraft in the U.S. airspace, and potential avenues for excluding portions of investigative reports. Their client eventually paired them with another firm with the expertise necessary to move the collective team further away from the origin of that three-axis system.

If cases are to be litigated in multiple jurisdictions, you will need to find quality lawyers in those jurisdictions who enjoy an excellent reputation among the judges and know the community. Local counsel can supply the context expertise of laws, judges, and jury venires specific to individual cases. Your local counsel should play a role in developing case-specific strategy and should have responsibilities at trial that take advantage of their skills, local knowledge, and reputation.

It's wise to select people for their differing skillsets, not because they're "just like you" but because they offer different perspectives. Learn to tolerate, embrace, and encourage those "not like you" who bring needed expertise and perspectives to your team.

There are circumstances, however, where you will not be in complete control of the choice of team members. Existing relationships between your client and other law firms may dictate the choice of local counsel. A contractual relationship with a service provider, perhaps a document management firm, may require that a particular group be chosen for an important task in the litigation. Nevertheless, the integration process will be similar.

[B] Build Trust

Once you've identified your team, you must build trust, a shared belief that you can depend on your teammates to achieve a common purpose. Team members must deal with conflict directly and fairly. Disputes about direction, roles, and recognition are inevitable in a collaborative relationship. Confronting issues and dealing with them not only resolves issues, but just as importantly, builds trust.

Earlier, when we discussed the need for courage, I said that a mark of that courage was the willingness of the team leader to have the hard conversations with team members. But have those conversations in private. If you must remonstrate do so privately, but celebrate achievements publicly.

When the leader sees a team member who is not sharing information, who is exercising sharp elbows, who is not putting forth the required level of effort, or who is not demonstrating the necessary level of competence to get the job done, a direct, private conversation is in order. Private conversations about performance avoid unnecessary embarrassment and damage to team morale.

I've found the following outline for such discussions to be effective:

- "I've got some information for you that will be disappointing to hear."
- "Here's what I see you doing that I view as contrary to the client's and team's interests."
- "Here's what I need you to do to correct this."
- "What are your thoughts about this?"
- "Are you willing and able to do this?"

Make it clear that if the person can't commit to a change in behavior or tries but fails to address the problem, you will have to remove them from the team. Give them a concrete corrective action plan they can respond to. Loop back to the team member later to give them a progress report on how they are doing. You hope the team member remedies the problem. After a chance to improve is given and progress is not being made, part of team building is team trimming when the circumstances require it.

[C] Define Team Goals

As we discussed earlier, clear definition of team goals is crucial. In Chapter 1, we talked about how those goals are established. Without clearly defined objectives, the milestones on the way to the accomplishment of the client's mission, the team has no focus.

Emphasize early and often that the path to achievement of the client's goals is through effective teamwork. A good team leader not only preaches teamwork, but models it as well. A good team leader also models a relentless pursuit of excellence, second best won't do and quality matters.

We sometimes forget as team leaders that our job is to set direction and empower team members to achieve the client's goals, not to micromanage their efforts. I sometimes fell into this trap, and had to remind myself to tell the team what I wanted done, not how to do it. As Gen. George S. Patton said: "Don't tell people how to do things, tell them what to do and let them surprise you with their ingenuity." If you try to tell team members how to do their job, I've found they will get the sense you don't trust them. They will become dependent on you or others for constant direction and may lose the individual initiative that separates highly functioning teams from those less capable. Once you give team members ownership of tasks, be available to consult, give them examples, follow up, exhort, and critique. But if you can, avoid disabling team members by taking over their jobs.[26]

[D] Encourage Communication

Lawyers can present unique leadership challenges in a team environment because they tend to be highly independent, competitive, aggressive, and introverted. Like all generalizations about categories of people, there are many exceptions to the personality type often associated with lawyers. And lawyers do have personality characteristics that are very helpful in a collaborative work environment because they tend to be thoughtful, energetic, creative, and caring. But lawyers frequently have trouble getting over themselves, and part of good team play is "checking the ego at the door." Communication about objectives, the status of the case, and next steps is a helpful antidote to internal competition. So, you should set clear priorities based on importance and urgency, then communicate those to the team members.[27]

Simple as it sounds, you can accomplish much through the practice of "leadership by walking around." I initially thought that walking the halls and checking in on team members was a waste of precious time. But when I began to do it, I began to connect better with the team members, understand who they are, what they're doing, how they're doing, and learn how I could help them succeed in the tasks they were assigned.

---

[26] Ken Blanchard and Spencer Johnston, *The One Minute Manager* (1986).

[27] More on how to do this when we discuss case management. Campbell, *supra* at 127.

I also found I was able to develop personal relationships with the team that paid dividends. It is difficult to be loyal to someone who is remote and unapproachable.[28] It is easier to do so when the team leader cares about you and what you're doing for the client. Let your team get to know you on a personal level.

Among the most important things leaders do is ask the right questions.[29] While you're walking around and connecting with team members, listen to those you are leading. Listening does not mean agreeing, but it does mean acknowledging what you've heard and caring.[30]

[E] Build Reward Systems

We frequently think of rewards in a law firm context as promotions to partner, increased monetary compensation, or opportunities for leadership of practice groups. But as Daniel Pink describes in his book *Drive*,[31] the secret to high performance and satisfaction is the deeply human need to direct our own lives, to learn and create new things, and to do better for ourselves and our world.

Your team will feel motivated if you train them in the skills needed to succeed in the litigation, and in the process grow their professional skills and fund of knowledge.[32] Training is preparation to succeed.[33] When you train your team members—best done before the litigation begins, but better done later than not at all—you are increasing the capabilities they bring to the client's case. You increase the human capital they can employ in their practices. The fruits of their human capital—called "capital rents" by economists—can be harvested on behalf of the client to improve outcomes in current and future engagements.

---

[28] Tom Peters & Robert H. Waterman, Jr., *In Search of Excellence; Lessons from America's Best Run Companies* (1982); Amy J.C. Cuddy, Matthew Kohut, & John Neffinger, *Connect, Then Lead*, Harvard Business Review (July–August 2013), https://hbr.org/2013/07/connect-then-lead.

[29] John Hagel III, *Good Leadership Is About Asking Good Questions*, Harvard Business Review (Jan. 8, 2021).

[30] Rabbi Jonathan Sacks, "The Spirituality of Listening," *Covenant & Conversation*, https://media.rabbisacks.org/20230730041710/The-Spirituality-of-Listening-Eikev.pdf (accessed Aug. 3, 2023).

[31] Daniel H. Pink, *Drive—The Surprising Truth About What Motivates Us* (2011).

[32] "Man's flight through life is sustained by the power of his knowledge." Inscription on Eagle & Fledglings Statue outside of Mitchell Hall, U.S. Air Force Academy.

[33] "Give me six hours to chop down a tree and I will spend the first four sharpening the ax." Abraham Lincoln.

When you invest in your team by training them to be better at their jobs, you equip them to succeed. You want to build case-specific skills that relate to the conduct of the current litigation, such as knowledge of the facts and law of the case, the personalities involved, and the way the team will conduct the litigation. You also want to build general skills that are not specific to any one case, but that have broad application and translate to other engagements. These involve knowledge of the rules of professional conduct, rules of procedure, rules of court, rules of evidence, and trial advocacy skills that will make your team members better lawyers in the long run. These skills are built through training, mentoring, and the opportunity to do the things trial lawyers do—write pleadings and briefs, argue to judges, meet with clients, witnesses, and experts, and participate in trials. In this way, you are building the human capital of the team members through training and experiences that will last them a professional lifetime. As I used to tell my partners and associates, you can lose a lot of things in your life, and sometimes things will be taken from you, but no one can take away the experiences you gain in your practice—that stays with you for a lifetime.

Being a part of the litigation team will also teach them the power of relational capital—the greater productivity, efficiency, and effectiveness that comes from the coordinated efforts of other members of the litigation team.[34] The training, mentoring, opportunities for new experiences, and shared work processes raise the performance of litigation teams. The client gains from your investment in higher productivity and greater efficiency. Your firm gains through higher client satisfaction and reputational enhancement.

After action reviews can also be viewed as training opportunities. I've found that these reviews are most effective when you drill down to examine why things went right and why things went wrong. Identify contributing factors; look for the root causes.[35] And do so with a healthy dose of humility (there's that word again). Then find ways to employ that knowledge in the next case.

One of the rewards law firm associates take from participation in trials and arbitrations is the opportunity to see how contested hearings are conducted. You can do this during trial by taking the time to gather the team to debrief about the day in court. What did you learn today? How can we do better tomorrow? Unfortunately, we seem to learn most

---

[34] Lewis, *supra* at 9–10.

[35] Campbell, *supra* at 108.

when things go wrong. So why not embrace what went wrong, and commit to doing better next time? And don't forget to celebrate what went right.

§ 3.06 RESILIENCE

An Air Force Academy classmate of mine who was a good college basketball player and is now a world-class basketball coach is reported to have a saying he uses with his teams to emphasize the importance of persistence and resilience: "Pound the Rock."[36] This is a way he tells his players to never give up. The first 100 blows on the rock may not split it, but the 101st just might. Don't quit. Keep pressing on.[37] This is a way of saying that while the lucky may enjoy instant success, the rest of us produce it through a history of trial and error, effort upon effort, upset and defeat followed by persistence and dedication to the task, and finally victory.

You want the team members to be gritty, and unafraid; as Col. (Ret.) Kim Campbell says, willing and ready "to turn into the wind."[38] But if you're running into a brick wall (admirable dedication to do that willingly, but perhaps not in the client's best interests to have you continue to do that at your hourly rate), perhaps it's time to reevaluate the strategy and try a different approach. Resilience comes from an attitude of confidence and commitment to the achievement of an ultimate objective, not a bull-headed insistence on a particular approach to that objective. There are several behaviors I believe contribute to the resilience of the team leader and team.

[A] Hard Work

Trial work is plain old hard work that can be mentally, physically, and emotionally draining. It is one of the most difficult things lawyers can do. But it also can be fun and immensely rewarding. With your client's permission, consider letting your team members take roles in the trial. This allows them to see both sides of trial work—the hard work along with the satisfying aspects. Even a few days in the courtroom

---

[36] Saying of Gregg Popovich, Coach, San Antonio Spurs of the National Basketball League, http://jackmalcomb.com, 2013/11 pound-the-rock.

[37] Campbell, *supra* at 16.

[38] Duckworth, *supra* at 245; Campbell, *supra* at 16.

watching what you do and how you do it will pay big dividends in terms of morale building and training. I suggest you model the level of dedication to the case you expect from your team members. Leading by example is the best way, in my view, to let others on the team know your expectations for them. When the team performs well, make sure they share in the rewards.

[B] Dedication to Excellence

If you expect to create an ethic of excellence in everything the team does, your job is to imprint on the team the belief that second best or just good enough doesn't cut it. Excellence requires a culture of continuous improvement which both creates and sustains the virtuous circle: effort, learning, result, better effort, more learning, better result.[39] This is a culture that values professional and personal growth and aids in the development of valuable skills. When you don't settle for anything short of excellence in the pursuit of your client's objectives, you are less likely to quit.

In an international arbitration involving a dispute between the owner and the operator of the largest polymetallic open pit mine in the world, our team would gather each evening at the close of evidence to post-mortem the events of the day and plan for the coming day. Everyone was very busy, but I found that spending a half hour together, and no more, to discuss what was learned from the day and what needed to be done for the following day was time well spent. Our client would sit in on these meetings. I would ask each team member what they learned that day and provide any coaching I could on that point. We'd then plan for the following day, and I would ask each team member what resources—human and otherwise—they needed to get their job done successfully. This little exercise gave the team the intended impression that I wanted them to grow professionally from the experience and to apply the new skills to the case at hand.

[C] Esprit de Corps

Esprit de Corps—team spirit—can help carry you and your team over rough spots, salve disappointments, and press past setbacks. If you

[39] Campbell, *supra* at xxi; Brene Brown, *Dare to Lead* 3–6 (2018).

demonstrate through your own behavior a sense of esprit de corps within the team, then each member will lift up others around them. High team morale creates resilience.[40]

Part of resilience is bouncing back when things don't go well. I had the privilege of co-trying a lengthy state court jury trial in a product defect case with one of my talented partners. The case involved a grisly set of injuries suffered by four plaintiffs, including a young man who had been rendered a quadriplegic. The product involved was in litigation in other jurisdictions as well, so our case was not a "one off." We knew that whatever the result, an appeal would follow and other cases around the country would proceed.

We succeeded in bifurcating liability and damages. The liability trial lasted about five weeks, then we recessed to await the jury's verdict on the question of liability. When the jury remained out for several days, my partner and I began to get that sinking feeling we would be putting on a defense to the damages portion of the plaintiffs' cases after all.

We gathered the team, told them what to expect, and turned everyone's attention from the hard work they'd already done to mount a liability defense to the preparation of witnesses and exhibits for the damages phase. We focused on the positive—our group of outstanding experts and the expected power of their testimony. When the verdict came in against our client on the first phase of the trial, we were ready to immediately proceed to put on a defense of the damages cases. No one was happy with the result in the first phase, but the team got up off the mat and quickly moved forward, acquitting themselves well in that second phase. They showed resilience—overcoming disappointment and meeting the challenge for the client. I was very proud of them for their grit and determination.

[D] Tolerance of Mistakes

Sometimes mistakes are made by you or a team member with the best of intentions. A good leader is tolerant of mistakes.[41] Give your team members freedom to stretch and to fail. "If you screw up, learn the lesson, don't do it again, and MOVE ON."[42]

---

[40] "Morale is . . . steadfastness and courage and hope . . . confidence and zeal and loyalty . . . elan, esprit de corps, and determination." General George C. Marshall.

[41] Jim Mattis and Bing West, *Call Sign Chaos* 45 (2019).

[42] Campbell *supra* at 41, 46.

Thomas J. Watson, Sr. was the President of IBM for 38 years in the early part of the 20th century when the company experienced meteoric growth and became one of the largest and most profitable companies in the world. There is a story that he once was asked if he intended to fire an employee who had made a mistake that cost the company $600,000, a substantial sum in that time. He replied: "No, I just spent $600,000 training him."

We all fail, but the best teams produce members that learn to "fail forward," learning from their mistakes or those of others, internalizing the lesson, then putting it behind them. Those that are afraid to fail are those who avoid challenges where they might fail. In doing so, they miss the opportunity to grow. Complex litigation is not a practice for the timid.

§ 3.07 TAKING CARE OF YOURSELF

Just as you take care of others as a leader, you also must take care of yourself. You are no good to your team if you're physically worn down, emotionally spent, and mentally exhausted. You no doubt have developed coping mechanisms to deal with the stress of litigation if you've reached the stage in your career where you are leading, or preparing to lead, teams in complex litigation. Nevertheless, let me offer a few observations that you might find useful.[43]

The law is one of three great learned professions recognized in medieval tradition; a high calling that rewards practitioners with a sense of accomplishment, service to others, and intellectual challenge. The law also has been recognized as a "jealous mistress" who requires "lavish homage," as Justice Joseph Story had it. The profession demands for success that any practitioner must, as Lord Eldon said, "work like a horse and live like a hermit." In other words, if you want to be a successful lawyer and team leader, you better be all in and ready to work hard. Fair enough.

But the profession can take a toll on its members that exceeds hard work. Many of the reasons for this emotional cost are self-inflicted. So,

[43] This discussion borrows heavily from an article published in the American Inns of Court's *The Bencher*, addressed to young lawyers searching for pathways to well-being in their chosen profession. Don G. Rushing & Andrew B. Serwin, "Pathways to Wellness in the Practice of Law," *The Bencher* 24 (Mar./Apr. 2020).

we must ask ourselves how we cope constructively with the stressors in our professional careers. How do we avoid negative wash-over effects from our professional calling into our personal lives? How do we do better at living both a professionally and personally fulfilling life? In short, how do we find that elusive greater good of "happiness" by minimizing the toll the profession in general, and high stakes litigation in particular, takes on us?

The first step is to understand the multi-faceted challenges we face as litigators. Here is my list.

- *Long working hours*: A 60 to 80-hour work week is not unusual. Lawyers sometimes are poor at taking needed rest breaks, including vacations, to refresh themselves from their demanding work schedules.
- *Client-generated pressures*: Demands for responsiveness, results, and cost-effectiveness ramp up the stress levels. A service ethic of "the client's always right" and "the client comes first" in an intensely service-driven profession sets very high expectations that are difficult to live up to.
- *Self-generated pressures*: We are good at putting pressure on ourselves. Personality types that seem to be attracted to the practice of law have a tendency toward perfectionism and a low tolerance for failure. We're hard on ourselves.
- *Self-doubt*: We sometimes entertain a sense of uncertainty whether we're doing the right thing and are reluctant to admit that doubt and seek help from others.
- *Competition*: Lawyers are competitive beings. We compete for clients, money, status, or "the win." The competition can feel, at times, unrelenting.
- *Professional isolation*: The law practice is frequently a solitary pursuit, inhabited by personalities that like to work independently.
- *Professional incivility*: A "dog eat dog" work environment, particularly among litigators, is all too common. Lawyers often act uncourteously toward one another. Courts are reluctant to step in and say, "enough is enough—stop it." And we aren't very good at policing the behavior of our own colleagues.

Given these challenges, what are some steps—prescriptions, if you will—we can take to address them?[44] You likely know many of these, but I suggest you consider the following.

℞ Seek professional help for depression, anxiety, substance abuse, suicidal ideations

Lawyers tend to have a strong need for control, and are reluctant to admit they need help.

They fear loss of control and confidentiality, and sometimes are so overwhelmed by the pressures they face that they feel there is nothing that can be done. Soldiering on in the belief you can "handle" the problem without the aid of others frequently isn't a winning strategy. There are resources available to lawyers that are just a phone call, email, or office visit away. Bar associations, both state and local, often provide counseling and support services for their members. Health plans typically cover periodic physicals and mental health counseling. Suicide hotlines provide lifelines to those experiencing extreme distress. If you suffer from these types of health problems, use the resources available to you.

℞ Move toward a state of happiness

The pursuit of happiness has consumed the thinking of our most gifted philosophers, is a central theme in some of the most important lessons of the Bible, and is one of the cardinal principles identified in our founding documents. In other words, it's pretty important. Happiness was viewed by Aristotle, for example, as a state which does not lack anything and is self-sufficient. Aristotle saw happiness as a goal of human life—seeking Eudaimonia—that involved a continuous effort to become the best possible version of ourselves. The Bible viewed happiness, called "*ashrê*," or "well-being," as living wisely according to God's plan. The Buddha summarized his teachings in one statement: "I teach only suffering and the end of suffering." Thomas Jefferson identified the pursuit of happiness (virtue), along with life and liberty, as an unalienable right in one of the greatest pieces of Enlightenment writing,

[44] Admiral William McRaven expands upon an address he made at a University of Texas graduation ceremony in a short book that encapsulates his suggestions for ways of dealing with hardship and overcoming challenges in life. William H. McRaven, *Make Your Bed: Little Things That Can Change Your Life ... And Maybe the World* (2017). This is an excellent addition to the suggestions I offer.

the Declaration of Independence. The fact these great sources of wisdom pondered this issue is a testament to its importance.

We can increase the joy experienced in life by becoming skilled, efficient, energetic, earnest, and learned in our profession, conscientiously protecting our livelihood and means of support for our families, and enjoying the company of virtuous, trustworthy, faithful family and friends. We also can increase our enjoyment of our profession and relieve some of the stresses that accompany an active trial practice by good communication with a spouse, a significant other, or a trusted friend about your challenges and recommended steps to well-being that are consistent with your pursuit of professional excellence.

℞ Set goals and frequently assess your progress

We can do ourselves a big favor by periodically taking the time to step back and reflect on where we are and where we're going. I'm not talking here about "to do" lists or action plans, but rather self-assessments that ask: How am I doing—really? How am I feeling about myself? Am I on the path I wish to pursue, or is this someone else's expectation for me? Am I helping others in a meaningful way? And perhaps most importantly, am I happy? And if not, why not?

℞ Take care of your spiritual side

Obviously, spirituality and religion are not the same thing. Whether or not one claims a religion, we all can cultivate our spiritual side. One of the best ways to calm the mind is to find a time for daily prayer, meditation, contemplation, and deep relaxation. Prayer and meditation quiet the mind, and allow us to empty ourselves and just listen for what's there. This is a time to seek help from a higher power to restore us to sanity when we feel we've gone a bit insane.

℞ Practice detachment in conflict

Conflict in the practice of law is inevitable. We operate in an adversarial system, whether we litigate or advise for a living, but many of these conflicts are not truly personal, even though they often feel like they are. How we manage the conflict is crucial to how our bodies respond. Professional detachment, a necessary first step, involves the separation of professional judgment on behalf of the client from the emotions of the situation.

Simply be present without judgment about whatever occurs. Just see what's there. Try to see difficult circumstances as learning experiences. Be the observer of your own professional role in the conflict, but do not internalize the conflict itself. Try to view whatever it is that is creating the conflict without avoidance or aversion. Observe how things are as you stand a bit outside of it. In other words, maintain good boundaries between your professional conflicts and your personal life.

℞ Commit to life-long learning

This may sound trite, but bears repeating. The legal profession is an invitation to life-long learning, intellectual growth, and the accumulation of knowledge. Commitment to a philosophy of "better next year" will yield rich rewards. Master your chosen area of specialty, but read broadly to enhance your fund of knowledge. In doing so, you'll increase in the wisdom that will position you better to help your clients, your family, your friends, and yourself.

℞ Take Good Care of the Machine

Just as you maintain equipment that helps you function in life, you also must maintain the principal piece of equipment that allows you to live life and practice law—your own mind and body. That means, among other things, learning to manage stress. The checklist for good personal maintenance is straightforward, but requires self-discipline to accomplish. Exercise, adequate sleep, and good nutrition are critical to coping with the demands of the profession. Non-legal pursuits that provide outlets for creativity, diversion from work, enrichment, and relaxation provide avenues to a full life.

With these leadership principles and examples in mind, let's next turn to effective management of complex litigation.

CHAPTER 4

MANAGING THE CASE

"There is nothing so useless as doing efficiently that which should not be done at all."

—Peter Drucker

Management is about setting direction to accomplish the announced vision for the client's case, creating orderly pathways in pursuit of the goal, and designing and implementing work processes to reach the goal in an efficient manner. Management involves control and direction of human and physical resources to achieve the team's objectives. In this chapter, we'll discuss approaches to the management of complex litigation that you can employ to optimize results for the client with the available resources. This chapter will be a bit lighter on the theoretical and a bit heavier on the practical.

I've found that effective litigation management is about manipulating several important "control levers" to make the team function smoothly, produce an excellent result, and hold down costs. As the lead lawyer, your ability to accomplish these objectives depends in large part on how well the team understands the mission and their roles in support of that mission, how effective the team is in developing shared work processes that aid productivity, and how successful you are in staying focused on the theme and theory of the client's case as the litigation proceeds. And perhaps most important, a good manager avoids tasks that should not be done at all. Turning over every rock to see what is under it is a waste of the team's resources and the client's money. Here are some tips on how to get this done.

§4.01 PROJECT MANAGEMENT PROCESS

As a starting point, let's envision the direction of a team in complex litigation as a project management process. Principles of project management are well-understood in business, and can be applied to and followed in litigation. A diagram of the typical project management process is shown below.

FIGURE 4-1

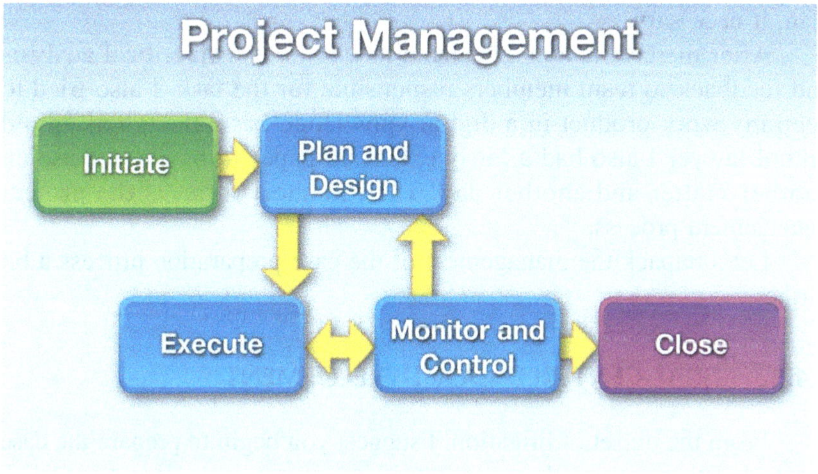

The initiation phase involves an understanding of the challenges to be addressed and a definition of the objectives to be achieved. I showed how this is done in litigation in Chapter 1. A plan that identifies the critical path from inception of the project to completion comes next. This is the creation of a "roadmap to victory" based on an early case assessment as outlined in Chapter 3.

Necessary tasks that must be completed along the litigation's critical path from filing of a complaint to judgment are listed, together with the resources to accomplish the tasks (lawyers, paralegals, consultants, experts, and the like), cost estimates for the tasks, and anticipated completion dates. This involves the preparation of an initial task list and strategic case budget of the type we also discussed in Chapter 1. We will return to the use of the task list in this chapter. Preparation of pleadings, motions, and discovery requests fall into the category of tasks to be planned. Importantly, this step is where you will begin to decide what potential tasks are worth doing because they will advance the client's interests in the litigation, and not worth doing because they are anticipated to yield low returns.

Once you identify the key tasks, the next step is to execute the steps you have identified as worth doing, for example a pleading, a motion, or a deposition. You will then monitor each task to determine if a quality work product is being created on schedule and on budget. As you monitor the completion of tasks and observe their effect on the litigation, you may need to respond to new information. This is the feedback loop between execution and planning that allows you to assess results and alter the plan, if necessary.

After the task is done, evaluate how it went with critical analysis and feedback to team members responsible for the task. I also tried to keep my work product in a digital knowledge base, though as an old school lawyer I also had a fairly extensive paper form file, for use on another matter and another day. This, in short form, is the project management process.

Let's unpack the management of the case preparation process a bit further.

§ 4.02 TRIAL-CENTERED CASE DEVELOPMENT

From the outset of litigation, I suggest you begin to prepare the case for trial. This may sound counter intuitive as most cases do not get tried, and precious few disputes ultimately are resolved through trial. The vanishing American trial is a reality. A very small percentage of criminal cases filed in the United States—about 2.5%—are tried to verdict. An even smaller percentage of civil filings result in trial—less than 1%.[1] But preparation of your case as if it *will* go to trial has several important benefits that inure to your client. First, if you prepare the type of strategic case plan I advocated in Chapter 1 that lays out your "roadmap to victory," your entire case workup will be planful, targeted, and efficient. Recall that your case preparation begins with the end in mind—what the judge will instruct the jury the law is (or will use to decide the case

[1] According to Judicature, in fiscal year 2022, approximately 1% of all civil cases filed in federal court were resolved by trial—the jury trial disposition rate is approximately 0.7%, and the bench trial disposition rate is even lower. According to the Pew Research Center, in fiscal year 2022, only 290 of 71,954 defendants in federal criminal cases—about 0.4%—went to trial and were acquitted. Another 1,379 went to trial and were found guilty (1.9%).

if it is a bench trial) and what you will say in closing argument about the facts of the case and how those facts compel a verdict in your client's favor. An efficient path in gathering the facts that matter and weaving them into a story that will resonate with the trier of fact prepares the case for both settlement and trial.

Second, if you develop a case theme of the type I advocated in Chapter 2 and relentlessly press that theme as a part of the story of your case in every phase of the litigation, you will educate your judge and your opponent about the reasons why your client ultimately will prevail in the case. To borrow a famous phrase from the 1969 American western "Butch Cassidy and the Sundance Kid," you will have your opponent asking: "Who are these guys?". This is a good way to drive a favorable settlement. Positioning your client for productive settlement discussions must be a part of your litigation strategy, and effective positioning begins with development of themes and a story arch that will resonate with the trier of fact.

Third, if you prepare a thorough issue outline of the type we will discuss later in this chapter, you will have organized the law and facts in a way that allows you to determine if there are dispositive motions, including motions to dismiss or for partial or complete summary adjudication, that will limit the scope of the case or end it. You will identify evidentiary motions that should be brought to ensure your key documents come into evidence and your important witnesses are able to fully testify. You will spot the motions to limit certain evidence your opponents will want to proffer. In short, your issue outline will both allow you to prepare your case for a reasonable settlement or, failing that, to try the case effectively.

All these steps will save the client money in the long run, will provide a high level of organization to your preparation efforts, and will avoid the chaos that leads to poor results. And if the case does go to trial, you and your client will be ready. There is little more distressing to clients than to find on the eve of trial that their law firm, which has worked on the case for many months, is not ready to try their case.

Your key tool for organizing the case in preparation for trial is the *trial notebook*. This is a physical object, in the form of one or more binders that can be taken into the courtroom, for us "old school" lawyers who like to have a hard copy to rely on. Or it can be a virtual object, for those digital natives comfortable with reliance upon computers, that is a collection of information accessible on a laptop that accompanies the lawyer to court. Whatever your preferred format, the trial notebook collects all case-critical information in one place. This is the destination for the work product created from the tasks assigned to team members during trial preparation. There is a place for the important things in it, and everything that is important has its place.

I suggest you start your trial notebook on day one and update and add to it as the case progresses. If you have a well-prepared trial notebook under your arm as you enter court to start trial (whether in notebooks or in digital files on your laptop), you and your team will do so with confidence you've done the hard work necessary to try the case successfully. And if you never wind up trying the case, you and your client will still benefit from the organization of the case into a trial notebook that collects the law, the facts, and the story line that explains the case in a single repository.

FIGURE 4-2

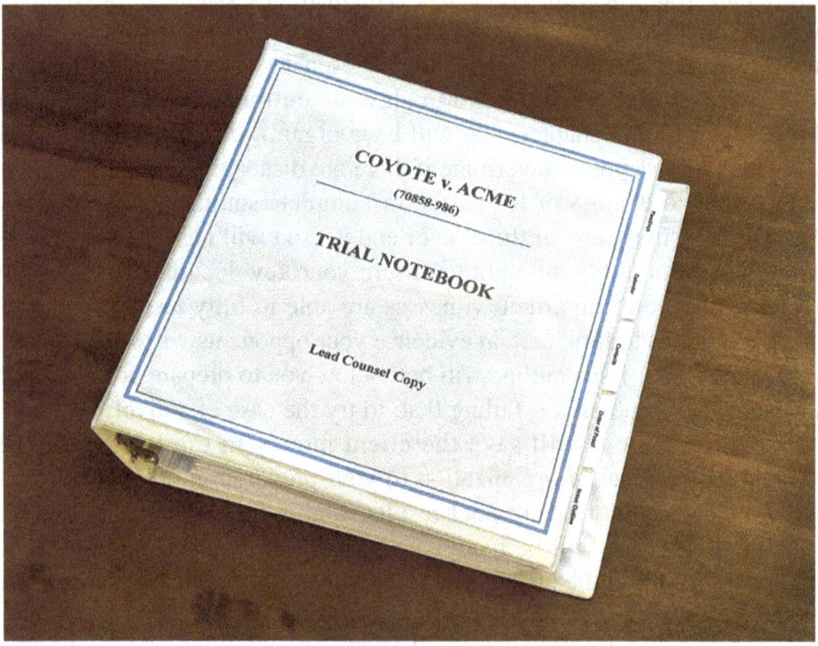

§ 4.03 THE TRIAL NOTEBOOK

For experienced trial lawyers, the concept of a trial notebook and what it contains is second nature. You likely have used this method of organization through many trials over several years and have your own ideas what to include in it and how to organize it. If so, treat this section as an *aide memoire*. If not, see if this approach is helpful in your case preparation.

Some of the tabs described below will be updated constantly as the case progresses and more information is gained (*e.g.*, contact lists, calendars, and task lists). Some tabs will be completed in later phases of the litigation (*e.g.*, experts and motions *in limine*). Some tabs won't be addressed until intensive trial preparation commences and the shape of the case is known based on completion of discovery and direction from the court about how the case will be tried (*e.g.*, a pretrial order, an order of proof, a trial time budget). But I suggest you begin to prepare your trial notebook at the outset of the case and continue to add to it throughout your preparation. Here are the "tabs" I think a complete trial notebook ought to contain.

[A] Contact List

This tab contains a list of all persons associated with the case, showing their name, address, phone number, email address, and role. Clients, client representatives, counsel, witnesses, experts, analysts, consultants, trial technologists, jury consultants, document management specialists, court reporters and videographers, court liaisons, and the court should be included. If you receive business cards from those involved in the case (a custom that is diminishing in practice, much to the regret of printers), it is often helpful to staple them to the contact list.

[B] Calendar

This tab contains a case-specific calendar of events. Court-assigned dates, statutory last days, discovery due dates, depositions, hearings, and the like should be shown on the calendar. Holidays and court "dark days" should be identified. In addition, witness availability dates for trial or deposition should be shown. When dates in the past are important, you also may wish to include printouts of blank calendars from previous years, so you know what day of the week a particular date fell upon.

[C] Task List

This tab contains a list of all items to be accomplished in trial preparation. This is your running "to do" list. Be specific about the "what," "who," and "when" for each task. Make the tasks discrete. Each task should have an owner—the person responsible for its completion. A clear due date should be assigned to each task. And a "status" section should be used to track progress.

Some lawyers find it helpful to subdivide their task lists by topic. Separate headings, for example, for pleadings, discovery, witnesses, experts, pretrial motions, and the like are often useful to further organize your trial preparation efforts.

A task list is your means of making sure that all that needs to be accomplished to be thoroughly prepared for trial will get done, nothing will fall through the proverbial cracks, your team members know who is responsible for a task, activities that do not advance the trial preparation are avoided, and work is not duplicated. The task list should be updated frequently as tasks are completed, and new tasks are added.

The team leader does not have to be the team member responsible for updating the task list; another person can be assigned the duty to track work projects and update the task list. And in very large cases, different team members might have responsibility for tracking the completion of tasks associated with different aspects of the case. Whether the team leader or another team member is the master of the task list, however, it is important for the leader to know the status of tasks assigned to others for completion and to monitor progress to make sure the team stays on schedule with case preparation. A typical task list is shown below.

FIGURE 4-3

Coyote v. ACME

PRETRIAL DEADLINES AND TASK LIST

Pleadings and Motions:

Task	Person Responsible	Due Date	Status	Comments
Prepare Motion to Exclude Plaintiff Expert Earl Austin	W.Janson; J. Simmons	2/11/19	DONE Filed 2/8/19	
Prepare Motion to Exclude Plaintiff Expert Brian Cutler	W. Janson; R. Moore (write research)	2/11/19	DONE Filed 2/8/19	
Prepare Motion to Exclude Plaintiff Expert Lisa Kraft	W. Janson; J. Simmons	2/11/19	DONE Filed 2/8/19	
Prepare Motion to Exclude Plaintiff Expert Louis Unger	F. Miller	2/11/19	DONE Filed 2/8/19	
Prepare Motion to Exclude Plaintiff Expert Charles Vinson	W. Janson; R. Moore	2/11/19	DONE Filed 2/8/19	
Prepare Summary Judgement Motion on Punitive Damages for Product Defect	F. Miller	2/13/19	DONE Filed 2/11/19	- Punitives - Preemption - Survival
Prepare Motion *in Limine* to Exclude subsequent remedial measures including post-accident product modifications	R. Moore; J. Simmons	2/18/19	DONE Filed 2/14/19	

1

[D] Issue Outline

This tab contains an outline of the elements of proof of the various claims in the complaint and affirmative defenses in the answer, regardless of which side of the case you're on. These elements come from pattern jury instructions you will have gathered at the outset of the case to understand the legal architecture of the litigation. The outline spells out the witnesses, documents, and physical and demonstrative evidence that you will use to prove or disprove each of the claims and defenses. This is your guidance for the preparation of the case and the conduct of a trial, and your main way of ensuring there will not be a failure of proof on a necessary element of the case.

The issue outline also frames in broad fashion the topics to be covered in witness examinations, and shows how documentary, physical, and demonstrative evidence will be admitted during the trial (*i.e.*, who the sponsoring witness will be for each piece of evidence). As you put together your witness examinations, the issue outline should be consulted to make sure you don't inadvertently leave out an area of questioning or the admission of evidence that is important to your client's case.

There is no magic to the format. The point is that elements of the case that must be proven by each side are matched systematically with the evidence—testimonial, documentary, physical, or demonstrative—that you will use to prove or disprove the element. Your issue outline also is useful in providing a detailed overview of the case. For this reason, it is a document that can be shared periodically with in house counsel managing the litigation for the client so they are kept informed of progress in the case and prepared to brief others within the company about the status of the matter.

[E] Cast of Characters

This tab contains a list of all persons who had a role in the underlying dispute, a description of who they are and what they did, and a notation whether a statement or deposition has been taken from them. Trials are like plays in that the people involved with the case have roles they play and become characters, the *dramatis personae*, in the dispute. Consider this tab your list of the characters that may appear as a part of the narrative in the trial, who simply appeared on documents that may be used at trial, or who may have been witnesses to or participants in some event relevant to the trial.

This list differs from the contact list we discussed earlier in that the people listed in the cast of characters are ones who have a direct role in the dispute underlying the litigation (*i.e.*, the witnesses). The primary purpose is to identify them rather than to contact them. Your cast of characters will also be of assistance when assembling a potential witness list for submission to the court as part of the pretrial proceedings.

[F] Chronology of Key Events

This tab contains a timeline of key events that includes a brief description of what happened and when. A chronology can be prepared by using word processing or spreadsheet software. There also are easy-to-use programs that allow your team to create visual timelines as the case develops.[2] As you progress to hearings, mediation, or trial, a graphic artist can create effective timelines of key events you wish to highlight in your presentation by reference to your chronology of events. Timelines allow your judge and jury to visualize the order in which events occurred and aid in answering the "what came first" and "what happened next" questions.

In all cases, but particularly in document-intensive cases, I have found it helpful to arrange key documents in chronological order and place them in digital or physical notebooks for easy review. The documents in effect create a timeline of key events and supplement the chronology you will create. Seeing the flow of events in the historical order in which they occur seldom fails to reveal new information and insights about the case.

[G] Pretrial Order/Key Pleadings

This tab contains the operative pleading in the case. In state court, this might be the last amended complaint, answer, and counter or cross claims that frame the remaining issues in the case. In federal court, this will be the final Pretrial Order, which supersedes the earlier pleadings and controls the course of trial. *See* Fed. R. Civ. P. 16(d) and (e). These documents are foundational to what evidence might be relevant in a trial. Keep them handy in your trial notebook.

[H] Witness List

This tab contains the party witness lists, or a joint witness list. In a federal court case, this list usually is included in the Pretrial Order entered by the court. The list of all witnesses to be called at trial should include a brief description of the substance of the testimony.

---

[2] A program I frequently used was CaseSoft's TimeMap® software, though there are others.

FIGURE 4-4

Coyote v. ACME

TRIAL WITNESSES

WITNESS	ROLE	DEPO DATE	DEPO EXH	Witness List	Resp. Atty	NOTES
AUSTIN, Earl	**Plaintiff's EXPERT-** Consumer Safety	10/19/18	1-15	P	CC	
BAKER, Peter	ACME Director of Production	5/15/18	1-9	P via depo video	RLF	
BANKS, Michael	**ACME EXPERT -** Design & Engineering	6/8/18	1-20	ACME	CC	
BARON, David	ACME Manager Production & Packaging	4/5/18	1-4	ACME	CC	
BEDINGER, Paul	Plaintiff's Friend	7/8/18	11-17 20-22	P	CC	
BRAGG, Ph.D. Martin	**ACME EXPERT -** Materials/Metallurgy	11/11/18	1-18	ACME	RLF	
CARLISLE, Eric	**ACME EXPERT -** Pyrotechnic Development	9/17/18	33-40			
CUTLER, Brian	**Plaintiff's EXPERT-** Accident Reconstruction	8/4/18	(Klurg 249-250)	ACME via depo	RLF	
DOYLE, Jackson	ACME ISO 9001 Compliance Administrator	2/7/18		P	CC	
ELLIOTT, Denise	Percipient witness, present at scene of incident	1/12/19	5-7	P	RLF	
GALLUP, Greg	**ACME EXPERT -** Safety Practices	4/29/18	1-7	ACME	RLF	
HANSON, Joshua	Percipient witness, assisted Sheriff at scene, former Fire Department Captain	5/25/19	158 - 163	RLF	CC	
HARRIS, Carlton	Percipient witness, present at scene of incident	12/28/18	2-18	ACME	RLF	
KRAFT, Lisa	**Plaintiff's EXPERT-** Metallurgy		11-14 27-30	P	CC	
McMASTER, Kyle	Paramedic Treated/Transported Plaintiff	10/22/18	19-24	P	RLF	
NORTH, Helen	ACME VP Quality Control	2/3/18	126-127	P	CC	
NORTON, Allan	Plaintiff's Accountant	6/19/18	7-12	P	CC	
PALLIS, M.D, Neil	Plaintiff's Physician	3/22/18	19-24 40-51		RLF	
RUSSELL, Mason	**ACME EXPERT -** Structural Analysis	8/9/19	1-10	ACME	RLF	
TRUMBO, Scott	ACME Mechanical Systems Manager	12/4/18 2/5/19	1-32 33-40	P via depo video	RLF	

1

[I] Expert Disclosures and Reports

Expert disclosures for all sides should be included in the trial notebook. A summary of expert opinions for both sides rendered in reports and during depositions also is helpful to include so that during trial testimony, opinions and conclusions that are offered but not properly disclosed may be objected to. Separate notebooks may be prepared for each expert to be called at trial, including expert reports, deposition summaries, outlines for direct and cross examination, and exhibits to be used with the expert.

[J] Exhibit List

This tab contains the parties' exhibit lists, or if the court requires sequential numbering of all exhibits as the court's exhibits, a joint exhibit list. I preferred to format this list with separate columns next to each exhibit showing not only the exhibit number and brief description (*e.g.*, "Ltr. on Acme stationary dated 9/2/2020"), but also any objections to admissibility, any rulings on admissibility, and dates on which the exhibit was offered and admitted into evidence. Our team checked this list daily against the court clerk's list to make sure the exhibits we thought were admitted into evidence indeed were, and to remind us of which exhibits needed to be moved into evidence.

An example of an exhibit list containing this information is shown below.

FIGURE 4-5

IN THE UNITED STATES DISTRICT COURT
FOR THE NORTHERN DISTRICT OF ARIZONA
PHOENIX DIVISION

COYOTE, ET AL. §
Plaintiffs §
§
vs. § **Civil Action No. 7:08-ES-1958-Y**
§
ACME INCORPORATED §
Plaintiffs §

DEFENDANT ACME INCORPORATED'S SECOND SUPPLEMENTAL TRIAL EXHIBIT LIST

EXHIBIT NUMBER	DESCRIPTION OF EXHIBIT	OBJECTING PARTY, IF ANY	BASIS FOR OBJECTION	IDENTIFIED	OFFERED	ADMITTED
217	5/12/18 ACME Engineering Summary Report re metallurgical lab testing results of modified 2706 quick release valve mechanism and brackets [2706-R-22]					
218	8/21/18 email from Scott Trumbo to Peter Baker re possible impact on 4th quarter production goals due to upcoming changes in materials					
219	12/13/18 email from Jackson Doyle to Mason Russell re updates to incident investigation report					
220	7/2/18 ACME internal sales report by state and region					

ACME'S SECOND SUPPLEMENTAL TRIAL EXHIBIT LIST - PAGE 57 5/20/2019

[K] Order of Proof

This tab contains a list of witnesses to be called in order, the trial team member responsible for their preparation and direct examination, and the estimated time allotted for the examination. In addition, anticipated witnesses to be called by opponents should be listed in a separate section, together with the trial team member responsible for cross-examination, if the witness is called, and a time estimate for the cross.

In organizing your case, rely on the issue outline for the witnesses you should call and topics you should cover. Changes to the court's schedule, witness availability, and other unforeseen factors may cause you to deviate from your order of proof, but having a good plan in place as a starting point is important.

I strived during the presentation of evidence to start strong and end strong. Pick a solid witness to begin your case who will carry the case theme and get you off to a good start. Use a strong capstone witness so you end on a high note. I tried to observe the rules of primacy and recency (the concept that a listener is most likely to remember the first and last things they hear) in ordering witnesses and outlining their examination. Pay attention to the chronology of events so your story, as told by the witnesses, flows in logical sequence.

There is no set way you should lay out your team's order of proof, but a typical format is shown on next page.

FIGURE 4-6

Coyote v. ACME
ACME's Tentative Order of Proof

1. Michael Maltese – ACME History
2. Helen North – ACME Quality Control Procedures
3. Scott Trumbo – (Video Depo) ACME Mechanical Systems
4. Martin Bragg, Ph.D. – Expert Materials and Metallurgy
5. Joshua Hanson– Former Fire Captain, Incident Witness
6. Greg Gallup – Expert ACME Safety Practices/Policies
7. Michael Banks – Expert Design and Engineering
8. Mason Russell – Expert ACME Structural Analysis Procedures
9. Bill Southworth – ACME Technical Writer Product Manuals
10. Carlton Harris - (Video Depo) Eye Witness to Incident
11. Peter Baker – ACME Production Techniques
12. Eric Carlisle – Expert ACME Pyrotechnic Systems Development
13. David Baron – ACME Packaging Practices
14. Susan Marsh, M.D. – ACME Medical Expert
15. Ron Marshall, Ph.D. – ACME Expert Economist
16. Virginia Parkin – ACME Training Policies
17. Jackson Doyle – ACME ISO 9001 Compliance
18. Olivia O'Dell – ACME Customer Relations
19. Noel Madison – ACME Expert Accident Reconstruction

[L] Trial Time Budget

If the court imposes time limits on the parties, a spreadsheet should be prepared showing each trial activity the court will count against your team's time. You won't know this until the pretrial conference, so preparation of the time budget will be one of the last tasks you undertake before the start of trial. List the trial phase (*e.g.*, lawyer conducted *voir dire*, opening statement, witness examinations), the witnesses to be called, the time you plan to allot to the activity, and how much time your team actually spent on the activity. Most judges who impose time limits on a case are serious about holding the sides to their time budgets. I have had judges tell the parties at the outset of a case how much time they were given to make arguments and examine witnesses, then have their clerk use a chess clock to record the time spent by each side. As one judge told the parties in a federal court trial I was involved in: “When your time is up, you’re done talking and will sit down.” I’ve seen experienced trial lawyers who are forced to hurry through their last witnesses and who are left with insufficient time for closing argument or rebuttal because they did not plan well. The time budget is your tool for avoiding this circumstance.

If you find yourself operating under court-imposed time constraints, it behooves you to check with the clerk or other court liaison who is recording the time how much of your side’s time you’ve used. Then, you can modify your presentation plan to make sure you leave enough time for important witnesses and, of course, closing argument. Your trial time budget is a vital tool to keep your team on track.

FIGURE 4-7

Coyote v. ACME
USDC, Northern District of Arizona
Case No. 7:08-ES-1958-Y
D/A: 7/4/17

Trial Time Allocation

Phase/Witness	Witness Role	Responsible Attorney	Allocated Time (hr.)	Actual Time	Difference	Comments
Michael Maltese	ACME company history	RLF	1.0		0	Live
Helen North	ACME quality control procedures and product testing protocols	CC	1.75		0	Live
Scott Trumbo	ACME mechanical systems	RLF	1.25		0	Video
Martin Bragg, Ph.D.	EXPERT - ACME materials and metalurgy, testing and certification	RLF	2.5		0	Live
Joshua Hanson	Percipient witness, former fire dept. captain, assisted Sheriff at scene of incident, weather/conditions at scene, observations of injuries	CC	.75		0	Live
Greg Gallup	EXPERT - ACME safety practices/policies, safety history	RLF	3.0		0	Live
Michael Banks	EXPERT - ACME design and engineering standards	CC	2.75		0	Live
Mason Russell	ACME EXPERT - ACME structural analysis of subject product	RLF	1.5		0	Live
Bill Southworth	ACME technical writer of operating manuals for consumer products - re revisions following product upgrades and/or changes to materials		1.25		0	Live
Carlton Harris	Percipient witness, saw incident and took 3.5 minute video (exhibit 125) immediately thereafter	RLF	.5		0	Live
Peter Baker	ACME production techniques, proprietary methods, and patent history of key products	RLF	2.5		0	Live

Page 1 of 3
Updated as of 7/8/2019 22:54 PM

[M] Chambers Conference

This tab contains material to assist you during your pretrial chambers conference. Consult your judge's local rules to determine likely topics to be covered during the chambers conference. This is the place in your trial notebook where you can store your notes on various topics that may be discussed with the judge during the conference. Typical topics include the following:

- Whether settlement has been explored and whether further discussions mediated by a judicial officer or private mediator might prove fruitful in resolving the case;
- Whether issues can be narrowed by stipulation or motion;
- Whether stipulations of facts can be agreed to reduce trial time;
- Trial time estimates, time budgets, and court calendar issues;
- Disposition of non-appearing parties;
- Dismissal of counts, defenses, cross-actions, or liens;
- Anticipated orders of proof and duties of parties to give reasonable advance notice of witnesses to be called;
- Seating of counsel in the courtroom;
- Courtroom logistics and technology;
- Lodging of depositions and discovery responses to be used at trial;
- Management of exhibits, including marking and control, witness and bench exhibit notebooks, stipulations regarding admissibility, use of copies, and passing exhibits to or displaying exhibits before the jury;
- Legal or evidentiary issues to be determined before trial;
- Jury issues, including the use of a jury questionnaire, judge- and counsel-conducted *voir dire*, the time to be allotted to each side for *voir dire*, examination of jurors at sidebar on sensitive issues, the size of the jury panel, the number of alternates, and the method of exercising challenges for cause and peremptory strikes;

- Production of adverse party employees for examination, use of interpreters, and fact and expert witness sequestration; and
- Trial day schedule.

[N] Motions *in Limine* and Rulings

The court has inherent power to exercise reasonable control over the conduct of the trial, including the order and manner of presentation of evidence, the mode and order of examination of witnesses, and the exclusion of evidence deemed irrelevant, lacking in foundation, or unduly prejudicial. Preliminary evidentiary issues that are ill-suited to determination during trial, and especially in the presence of the jury (*e.g.*, material that is unduly prejudicial), should be raised by motion before the commencement of trial. Included in this category are motions to apply foreign law and to have facts determined to be without substantial controversy.

For the heavier motions where significant briefing occurred, our team typically prepared separate notebooks for each motion *in limine*, including the motion and supporting memoranda of points and authorities, any reply or responding papers, and any relevant exhibits or transcripts. Once rulings are obtained, a summary of *in limine* rulings should be placed in the trial notebook along with a copy of the ruling.

Team members, the client, and witnesses should be briefed carefully on court rulings to ensure compliance with the court's orders. This is particularly important with witness exclusion orders under provisions such as Federal Rule of Evidence 615. In addition, anticipated motions to be made or responded to during trial, key arguments, and drafts of motions or oppositions should be included in this tab.

[O] *Voir Dire* and Juror Profile

This tab contains a summary profile of favorable and unfavorable juror characteristics, attitudes, values, and beliefs. A juror profile can be prepared based upon formal jury research with mock juries, as the example shown below demonstrates, or more informal focus group work. The team's analysis of the issues, evidence, and themes also can substitute for more formal jury research. The juror profile will provide the "yardstick" against which members of the jury *venire* are assessed for challenges for cause or for peremptory challenges during *voir dire*. The juror profile also serves as a guide to the types of questions you should be asking of the jury *venire* during *voir dire*. Also included in this tab is a list of questions you will request that the trial judge ask in lieu of party *voir dire*. You can develop a simple "favorable" and "unfavorable" list of factors from this raw data to use during jury selection as you *voir dire* the panel.

FIGURE 4-8

	Income						Political Affiliation		
Issue	<$15,000 (4)	$15k-25k (6)	$25k-35k (2)	$35k-55k (4)	$55k-75k (5)	$75k-100k (2)	Rep. (7)	Dem. (3)	Ind. (3)
Plaintiff Verdict	0	4	0	0	0	0	2	0	0
Defense Verdict	4	3	2	4	5	2	5	3	3
descriptions/limits/procedures not clearly defined in manual	0	5	0	0	1	1	2	2	0
position would change if Coyote was properly trained/warned	2	0	0	0	3	1	2	1	1
safety standards re manufacturing and training a priority	0	0	1	0	2	1	0	1	1
found precautions to be important/persuasive	0	0	1	1	2	0	1	0	1
history to be persuasive (voted for Plaintiff)	0	3	0	0	0	0	2	0	0
Accident history raised red flags/wanted more info on accidents (voted for Defense)	1	2	0	1	3	1	0	3	0
thought ACME should provide more training re weather factors	0	3	0	1	0	0	1	0	0
poor planning/ignoring weather bulletin persuasive	1	3	0	0	1	0	3	1	0

If a juror questionnaire is permitted, consider taking key information about jurors from the questionnaire and including it in questions you have for specific jurors. A jury seating chart showing juror number and name, a juror profile listing desirable and undesirable characteristics for your case, a list of questions for jurors based on their questionnaire responses, and a list of challenge for cause grounds and objections to opponent strikes may also be in this tab.

Every trial lawyer has their own way of organizing *voir dire,* tracking responses, and deciding whether to exercise challenges. I began each *voir dire* with a clear idea in mind what type of juror I would want to deselect from the panel and what type of jurors I would want to protect from challenge because they likely would be favorable—a juror profile.

A method I sometimes employed involved a chart of the jury box and Post-it® notes with the name and number of the juror and information about that juror on the note. The notes could be moved around as jurors were seated and excused. Jurors who I wished to challenge for cause were marked with a red "C" along with a brief notation what the basis of the cause challenge was. Those jurors who were possible peremptory challenges were marked with a blue "P." If you have a trial consultant, in my experience this portion of the trial is where they prove to be most helpful.

[P] Key Discovery Responses

Copies of interrogatory answers and requests for admission responses to be read into evidence are included in this tab. If deposition excerpts are to be read to or played for the jury by video, designations from the applicable depositions may also find a home in this tab.

[Q] Opening Statement

As the case develops, you should make notes on themes to be announced and possible exhibits to be displayed in opening to begin to educate the jury about your client's case. When ready for trial, this tab will contain your outline for the opening statement. As we discussed in Chapter 2 on the importance of storytelling in effective trial advocacy, I am a strong believer in outlining—not writing out—the opening statement and identifying the exhibits you will use in your opening. This tab is where you should place your outline and the exhibits the court will allow you to use in your opening statement.

[R] Witness Outlines

In complex litigation, you simply will not have enough room for all your witness examination outlines in one notebook. I preferred to have separate notebooks for each witness. Each witness notebook should include an examination outline, a copy of exhibits to be used with the witness, a copy of any statements made by the witness, and a deposition summary. List anticipated objections to witness testimony and responses to the objections with cites to rules, cases, or statutes. For expert witnesses, include a copy of any reports and expert witness designations.

[S] Closing Argument

As the case develops, notes on themes and key points to be covered can be kept here. At trial, the outline for the argument, including references to exhibits or trial testimony to be displayed will be stored in this tab. As with your opening statement, don't write out your closing argument. Instead, outline the key points you want to make, annotated with exhibit references. This will give you confidence you won't forget to cover important evidence, and allow you to engage with the jury in a conversational tone.

[T] Jury Instructions and Verdict Form

During case development, the core jury instructions that set out the law on various claims and defenses and a draft verdict form will be kept here. At the beginning of a case, I was in the habit of pulling the applicable jury instructions so I knew what each side had to prove to prevail. These instructions provided the legal architecture for the issue outline.

Once the court has settled the jury charge, substitute a copy of the final version to be read to the jury for the ones you selected at the outset of the case. Likewise, when the verdict form has been settled, substitute the final version for the draft you worked from as you developed the case. I have found it handy to have an extra copy of the verdict form in this tab to mark up as the verdict is read by the foreperson.

[U] Post-Trial and Appeal

This is a place for notes during trial concerning rulings that may form the basis for post-trial motions or issues on appeal. In complex litigation, I routinely consulted an appellate lawyer to make sure I correctly identified potential appellate issues and took appropriate steps to preserve those issues for appeal.

Those, then, are the building blocks of a good trial notebook. As I mentioned earlier, the preparation of a trial notebook is, by nature, an iterative process. As you learn more about your case, complete discovery, find witnesses, review documents, and identify potential trial exhibits, retain and work with experts, engage in motion practice, and conduct jury research, the contents of your trial notebook will grow and change. The trial notebook is not static. While it resembles a library in some respects as a repository of useful information, it is a changing collection of important information that will aid you in trial.

You want to encourage your team to be creative in developing the case for trial, and in funneling that work product into your trial notebook. This will result inevitably in changes in the contents. There is a tension, however, between creativity and efficiency. The creative instinct is to modify, tweak, and iterate to make your work better, whether you are writing, painting, composing music, gardening, or—yes—preparing a trial notebook. But to change, and change, and change again without reaching completion takes creativity too far in trial practice. *At some point, the search for perfection becomes the enemy of the good.*[3] A hearing or trial date will arrive. When that time comes, your team will want to have solid work product to use. No last-minute scrambling because the work product still is being tweaked.

Step back from the daily pressures of the case periodically to remind yourself what your story is, what your themes are, and what new information you've learned that might alter your view of the case. Don't get buried in the trees. Look at the forest occasionally. You'll gain perspectives that otherwise would have been missed.

Finding the balance between creative case approaches and practical, goal-oriented trial preparation is an important function of the case manager. I found that an aspect of my job as the lead trial lawyer was to judge at what point further "fine tuning" of our preparation had reached a point of diminishing returns. I did this in consultation with the client. When that point was reached, it was my job to call a halt to the effort.

Pareto's 80/20 Rule is at play here, as it is in other contexts. Your team can continue to find and analyze documents and interview secondary and tertiary witnesses in a search for additional lines of examination or argument—the 20% in Pareto's Rule—but at some point, the benefits of this additional effort simply are not worth the time and expense. Will you really use this information or call those witnesses at trial? Does the added work really advance the case? If the answer is "probably not"

[3] "Perfectionism is the voice of the oppressor, the enemy of the people. It will keep you cramped and insane your whole life, ... I think perfectionism is based on the obsessive belief that if you run carefully enough, hitting each stepping-stone just right, you won't have to die. The truth is that you will die anyway and that a lot of people who aren't even looking at their feet are going to do a whole lot better than you, and have a lot more fun while they're doing it." Anne Lamott, *Bird by Bird: Some Instructions on Writing and Life* (1994).

you've reached a stopping point. In my view, the quality of trial preparation is measured not only in the thoroughness and thoughtfulness of the effort, but the cost associated with the preparation.

Let's turn next to two key building blocks of your case, technology solutions that knit the team together and allow for the efficient management of documents, and expert witness retention and development. In addition to the importance of a good graphics program to provide the visual element to the story (discussed in Chapter 2), the team leader needs to make sure at the outset of a case that shared technology and document management, and the development of expert witness testimony are being attended to.

§ 4.04 SHARED WORKSPACES AND TECHNOLOGY USE

From the outset, you should deploy technology that makes information easily accessible to the team and is a reliable internet-based resource for case information. This technology knits the team together, even if team members work remotely from one another. Access to shared data bases allows team members in various geographical areas to work together on document reviews, trial exhibit identification, and reviews of discovery responses and deposition testimony. Shared digital databases make access to information fast and inexpensive. This, in turn, makes the team more productive.

I probably am "preaching to the choir" of younger lawyers who came of age in an era of ubiquitous use of computers, the internet, and document management software. But some lawyers are reluctant to use technology, or to try new things until forced to do so by client and cost control needs. Computer-based document review and management systems are crucial to efficient document production in discovery and identification of trial exhibits as trial approaches. And I should express here my concern that as soon as my observations about current litigation support technology are published, they will be dated because of the rapidity of change in this area. For this reason, I'll keep my suggestions on a conceptual level.

As the Model Rules of Professional Conduct have evolved, there also is an ethical obligation to stay abreast of and use technology for your client's benefit. Since 2012, American Bar Association Model Rule 1.1 dealing with the lawyer's duty of competence includes in a comment the notion that competent handling of a particular matter includes the use of methods and procedures meeting the standards of competent practitioners. For those handling the most complex of litigation matters, this necessarily includes competence in the available technological tools to make your litigation team efficient and effective in the management of documents and other evidence developed in the case.

I confess I'm not savvy enough about these technological systems to do justice to their description. When I took my first computer science course in 1967, the computer language was ALGOL and the computer processing the punch cards containing the programming commands filled a good part of a large room. In business school in the early 1970's, the computer language had advanced to Fortran, another first-generation programming language, and the computer was only slightly smaller. A lot of water has passed under the bridge when it comes to computer hardware and software. I was content to leave the highly technical area of computer-based litigation support to experts in the field, but to understand enough about it to know how to employ it in support of the litigation and to know to whom I could turn to field the technology for my client. I am convinced that while as the team leader you do not need to understand all the nuances of the technology your team fields to manage the case, it is necessary for you to be a *capable user* of that technology.

Litigation support technology useful to the management of complex litigation, especially when more than one law firm or one office of a single law firm is involved in supporting the client, includes *information sharing software* (*e.g.*, eRooms that store documents, discovery, and pleadings), *document review software* that aids in the gathering, review, and production of documents, and *trial support software* that takes trial graphics, deposition testimony, and documents into the courtroom with the trial team. I do not advocate for any particular type of software for information sharing, document management, or trial support. There are several good resources to accomplish these tasks.[4]

Some firms find and retain a highly skilled provider of these services to rely on at the outset of complex litigation. Some firms embrace and invest in their own document management specialists and computer infrastructure, building out their own "end-to-end" eDiscovery and trial technology departments with dedicated computer experts

[4] *E.g.*, from a discovery management perspective, "Relativity" is a document review system, though by no means the only system, commonly used in litigation that allows multiple users simultaneous access to the data base. Whatever system you choose, the system selected to support the team should be "end-to-end" capable (*i.e.*, from location and gathering of documents from the client to production to the opponent and court), and should be supported by a competent, responsive service provider.

leveraging software and hardware the firm has procured or created. Some have elected a smaller personnel and infrastructure footprint with a skilled technologist establishing relationships with and directing outside service providers. Whatever solution you settle on, however, putting in place people and systems to help you and your team through the thicket of eDiscovery and document management is crucial to your success in serving your client in complex litigation.

Document databases that allow for remote document review to determine the responsiveness of documents to discovery requests, screening for potential privileges, witness preparation, or potential use as a trial exhibit particularly have benefited from recent advances in generative Artificial Intelligence (AI). AI-driven workflows that involve computer analytics to build data bases of documents based on the requirements of the user without manual input from a litigation team member have improved the speed and reduced the expense of document reviews.

Technology Assisted Review, an application of AI in litigation support, is now able to take a "seed set" of statistically valid documents from lawyer reviews and apply them to new documents sets. As new sets are created, they are rated by reviewers for accuracy, improved instructions are given, and the computer software self-corrects or "learns" in an iterative process. The objective is for attorney document reviews to agree with computer reviews on a level of frequency that court, client, and attorneys accept as accurate. When the "machine" gets it right most of the time, human document reviewers are relieved of the drudge work associated with endless hours of document review.[5]

Newer technology is beginning to apply Computer Assisted Learning (CAL) that makes determinations without a "seed set" and based on criteria created by an attorney. In the background of the review process, as reviewers agree or disagree with the computer, the computer updates all the documents previously reviewed based on the new criteria. CAL can also be used as a quality control and quality assurance technique for human and computer document reviews. Discovery is the most expensive part of any litigation. The application of computer based tools to make the discovery process efficient is a must.

Once discovery is completed, your team will need an Application Programming Interface to "bolt on" the documents you choose from the

[5] According to Andrew Bayer, CED, RCSP, a Managing Shareholder of Consilio, human reviewers have error rates of 15–20%, so a reasonable goal for computer decision making is about 85%.

document management system to another program used for trial support (*e.g.*, Sanction® or Trial Director®). A good trial technologist who knows how to use these systems is crucial to take the fruits of pretrial efforts into the courtroom and to provide the visual dimension of advocacy.[6] There is a cost, to be sure, associated with the software applications, but they are time savers for the most expensive resources in any litigation, the lawyers, paralegals, and analysts who work on the case.

I hope I have sketched in broad outline the categories of technology support that will make your litigation team efficient and effective. The tools available to you as a team leader will change over time, and change rapidly. The development of large learning models and AI continues to make major gains in sophistication and usefulness and fundamentally will change how cases are litigated in ways I cannot predict. In an age where shared technology enables greater speed and productivity in litigation, it is imperative as a good team member to become proficient in using these valuable tools. Your goal should be to stay on the cutting edge—hopefully not the bleeding edge—of this rapid innovation.

§ 4.05 EXPERT WITNESSES

Complex litigation typically involves the heavy use of consultants and experts. This is a natural feature of the scientific, engineering, medical, technical, and economic complexity of these cases. You will need professionals as a part of your litigation team who are able to explain, to teach, and to guide both the lawyers working on the case and the judge and jury. I suggest you begin to locate, retain, and educate your experts on the facts of the case from the very beginning of your engagement as counsel. They are one of the vital building blocks of a successful case.

[A] Functions of Consultants and Experts[7]

Lawyers who handle sophisticated matters for their clients usually are well grounded in the ways experts are used in litigation. Consider my suggestions as reminders of their importance.

[6] Sanction® and TrialDirector® are presentation software systems that allow the assembly of documents, exhibits, transcripts, visuals, and videos to display evidence during hearings and trials.

[7] I use the term "consultant" to describe a person with expertise in a discipline important to the litigation who has not yet been or will not be designated as a testifying witness

One important function of consultants is to *advise and teach* lawyers about their case. Frequently, complex litigation centers on sophisticated technologies that are unfamiliar to lawyers. When that occurs, help from outside experts is necessary to equip the litigation team with the necessary understanding of the technology underlying the dispute. There are, of course, exceptions. I benefited on several occasions from technical expertise within my own firm.

In several intellectual property cases, I had partners and associates with doctoral degrees in biochemistry and genetics who were able to fill the role of "educators" about the science of the case. In other cases, I had the benefit of a former Air Force pilot with thousands of hours of multi-engine jet flight experience, a master's degree in Aeronautical and Astronautical Engineering, and an FAA Airline Transport Pilot Rating who served this role. But these internal resources are the exception rather than the norm. When you don't have them, you need to look elsewhere.

I fell off the Chemistry wagon at Chemistry II in undergraduate school. When I became involved in patent litigation over polyimide and polyamide foam technology, I found I needed help to understand the Organic Chemistry involved in the dispute. I located that help in a local college professor. The professor was good at explaining difficult concepts to our team in relatively simple terms. We used the professor solely as a teacher of the basic science and consultant on the art taught by the relevant patents, and not as a potential expert. This allowed us to freely communicate about the science and ask questions of him without fear of compromising his objectivity if he also served as an expert. The professor also was able to conduct tests of alternative formulations for us without concern that the results of the tests would have to be disclosed in discovery.

Experts also aid in *clarifying, focusing, and framing issues* in the case. They can bring order to the chaos that can surround complex cases by helping to identify key technical issues and explaining how those issues fit into the overall architecture of the case. What might seem important to a layperson learning the facts of a case might seem unimportant or even irrelevant to an expert in the area. This point was brought home to me in a series of alleged toxic exposure cases where plaintiffs claimed injuries due to ingestion of a chemical found in their well water. The description of possible toxic effects from exposure to the chemical

---

in a case. Ordinarily, consultants can remain under the attorney work-product protection during litigation, but experts, once designated, cannot. Fed. R. Civ. P. 26 (b)(4)(D).

sounded dreadful. Once our expert quantified the potential exposure levels and related that exposure to background environmental exposure levels, however, it became apparent that the case was more about the level of exposure rather than the characteristics of the substance to which the plaintiffs were exposed. To bring home this point, our expert took samples of water from a drinking fountain outside of the courtroom where the case was to be tried and compared it to levels in the well water. They were roughly the same.

Consultants and experts also can be very helpful in *assisting in discovery*. Their aid in crafting interrogatory questions, document production requests, and requests for admission can be invaluable because they are able to suggest sophisticated questions that target important issues in the case or lead to key facts. Your experts can also aid in the preparation of outlines for the taking of depositions. I routinely involved my experts in deposition preparation, asking their help in suggesting areas of examination. I also frequently took my expert or consultant with me when examining technical witnesses or opposing experts so they could listen with a trained ear to the answers and suggest follow-up questions. Use your experts to enhance the quality of your discovery.

Experts have a role to play in *Daubert motions* that seek to limit or prevent the testimony of opposing experts. Attacks on the qualifications, factual foundation, or principles and methods used by an opposing expert frequently will be supported by the declaration of your own expert. This will require detailed review of both the opposing expert's report or statement of opinion and the deposition testimony of that expert. Motions *in limine* attacking opposing experts are expensive and time-consuming to prepare, and should not be embarked upon casually. But your own expert can help you determine if there is a realistic chance of success, and on what grounds.

And of course, experts can provide necessary testimony in a hearing or trial to prove the elements of a claim or defense. If, in the words of Federal Rule of Evidence 702, scientific, technical, or other specialized knowledge will assist the trier of fact to *understand* the evidence or *determine a fact in issue*, an expert may be used to provide testimony on those points. Moreover, the expert may give an opinion on the ultimate issue in the case in federal courts.[8] This is a big advantage to the side with the strong, well-qualified, well-prepared experts.

---

[8] Fed. R. Evid. 704.

Your own experts also can be used to "cross-examine" the opposing experts by putting questions to them that frame the testimony of the opposing expert and asking for their response. You examination of your own expert might read something like the following.

"Q: Sir, Ms. Smith testified that the observed concentration of the chemical in the laboratory area was in the range of 0.50 parts per million on an 8-hour time-weighted average. Assuming that's correct, is exposure at that concentration potentially hazardous to humans?"

A: No

Q: Please tell us why that's so.

A: NIOSH guidelines permit levels of exposure in the workplace that are substantially higher than that.

Q: If Ms. Smith said otherwise, would she be correct?"

A: No, she would not.

Q: Why not?

A: No toxicology study I am aware of has ever shown adverse effects in humans from exposures at the levels she claims to have measured in the laboratory area."

It often is easier to get straight answers out of your own expert by way of this method than by verbally wrestling with an opposing expert to get to the same conclusion, as much fun as that might be.

[B] Expert Selection and Development

We all have a picture in our mind's eye of the characteristics of the ideal expert. When I list these characteristics, I have in mind the three experts that I felt best exemplified what an effective expert should be. Here is my list:

- They were *highly qualified* in their fields, and had excellent credentials. Look for people with a strong background in your field of interest, whether their qualifications come from academic studies, work experience, teaching, or publications.
- They were *independent* minded, coming to their own conclusions. They did not allow lawyers to tell them what they should

say. They made up their mind about a subject after study and analysis of the facts.

- They were *thorough* in their preparation. If they needed information or materials to adequately form their opinions, they asked for it and I made sure they would get it if it was available.
- They were *balanced*; they did not stretch to try to make a point. They avoided overstatement. They responded directly to questions from opposing counsel (no ducking and dodging) and showed great respect for the court.
- Their testimony was *lucid*—clear, straightforward, and to the point. They were able to use examples and analogies to illustrate their testimony.
- They were *honest*; they told the truth. They avoided equivocation.
- They were *experienced* as expert witnesses, but not shop worn or unduly identified with a client, law firm, side, or litigation position. Retention of a well-qualified expert who has never served in the role of an expert witness in litigation has the advantage of minimizing a claim of bias, interest, or other motive,[9] but increases the time you will need to spend with the expert to prepare them for effective testimony.
- They made themselves *available* for consultation, preparation, and testimony. Hiring someone who is too busy to spend time on your case is pointless.
- They were *consistent*; they did not change positions without a very good reason.
- They were *charming* on the witness stand, able to tell a story, and tell it well. (Pity none of them had an English accent, as that would have added to the perception of their intelligence.)
- They exhibited uncommon *common sense*. No one was going to pull them into the *reductio ad absurdum* trap.
- Best of all, they were *correct* in their conclusions.

[9] *See* Fed. R. Evid. 607 and 608.

Where do you begin your search for experts of this type? I looked for qualified teachers of the subject, preferably from universities in the area where cases were likely to be tried. An economics professor from a local college with a background in labor economics might serve equally as well as a professor from an elite institution from another part of the country in preparing an age earnings profile on a plaintiff claiming future economic loss, for example. But if the stakes are high enough, I would not let efforts to find someone local take precedence over someone who would be more effective in the case. As an example, we retained a Harvard labor economist and demographer to serve as an expert on lost earnings in a product liability case in lieu of other local economists because of his exceptional expertise, thoroughness of preparation, and ability to explain his methods and conclusions. Attempts by our opponent to portray him as a "carpet bagger not from these parts" fell flat in the face of his credentials and the force of his conclusions.

Our team also researched the relevant scholarly publications to find authoritative writers on a subject. A good research librarian, for example, often can turn up authors who published in academic journals on the very subject involved in your case.

We also looked for people who worked in the field and who had practical knowledge to share. On several occasions, we found pilots who flew the type of aircraft involved in an accident by checking with operators of the airplane to identify their chief pilot. In serial litigation regarding a building product, we located potential technical experts by learning who the installers of the product were in various jurisdictions. In a series of tire mismatch cases, we found articulate, experienced installers at local tire centers who could describe the dos and don'ts of tire mounting.

In intellectual property litigation, you might perform a prior art search to identify inventors of allied technologies. The inventors might serve as a starting point in finding people who can speak authoritatively in narrow areas of expertise.

Finally, you might search for people who won important awards, received acclaim, or are highly credentialed in an area relevant to the litigation. These are the "famous people." You don't hire them because they are famous, you hire them because they know what they are talking about and are known. But their notoriety can be a plus if they are otherwise well qualified. I tried an aviation product liability case many years ago where one of the witnesses was Apollo 12 astronaut Pete Conrad, one of the few people in history who walked on the moon. The reason he served as a witness wasn't because of his NASA experiences, but because of his knowledge of the product in suit and his important position with a company that was one of the defendants. It certainly didn't hurt his credibility that he was a famous astronaut.

One more point on the identification and retention of experts. Beware the professional expert, beware the all-purpose expert, and beware the professional expert mills. Witnesses of this type often suffer from positional bias—always testifying for the same side—or over exposure—testifying too often on a variety of subjects. This compromises their appearance of objectivity and makes them easy targets for cross-examination.

[C] Vetting of Experts

Careful background research should be performed on any expert you may consider retaining. This vetting process begins with the potential expert's credentials. Are they well qualified in the applicable field? Are you certain they possess the academic degrees they say they have? The work experience they list on their *curriculum vitae*? The publications they claim? When you don't do a thorough job of checking an expert's background and offer him to testify, the results can be embarrassing.

In a state court jury trial, one of several scheduled in serial product liability litigation, a damages expert was offered by the plaintiff to testify to lost earnings. The witness's website claimed he held a Ph.D. in Economics from an institution I attended at about the same time he claimed to have been a doctoral candidate there. I became suspicious of his credentials, however, when he didn't seem to recognize any of the professors from the Economics department of the school. We subpoenaed his transcript. The transcript showed up on the first day of trial, sealed in an envelope. During my cross-examination of the expert, the bailiff opened the envelope and handed me his school transcript. After everyone had an opportunity to review it, and the court confirmed the process for obtaining the transcript had been followed, it was admitted into evidence. By this time, the jury now suspected the transcript would be inconsistent with the expert's claims and was anxious to see what it said. We displayed the transcript on a big screen in the courtroom. The transcript revealed that the expert earned an M.B.A. from the university's graduate school of business—no shame there—but not a Ph.D. from the Economics department. This did substantial damage to the witness's credibility. The lawyer who hired him and put him on the stand seemed surprised at this turn of events. The message is "trust, but verify."

Before retaining an expert, you will want to learn of her prior testimonial history. Have they taken positions under oath or in filings with courts that commit them to a position that is contrary to positions you wish to advance in your case? Have they been consistent in testimony on issues that matter to your case?

A careful review of all previous writings on a subject should be undertaken. What have they said in writing or in videos about a topic? If they teach a subject, what do they say about it in their teaching? Is the potential expert's writing and teaching consistent with your case theme and the position you wish to take in the litigation? If not, better keep looking.

If a potential expert had worked previously for other lawyers, I made it a habit to call and talk with those lawyers. I wanted to learn how easy the expert was to work with, how diligent in her preparation, how effective in organizing thoughts on the case into a coherent opinion, and how effective on the witness stand. You can learn a lot about experts by asking those who have worked with them on other occasions.

I recommend, if possible, you have a face-to-face meeting with a potential expert before retaining them. What impression does she make in person? Do you find her likeable, articulate, and knowledgeable? Does she have an interest in serving as an expert in your case? Does she have the time to commit to your case, and a willingness to do so? What is her hourly rate, is it reasonable, and how does it compare with compensation she receives for services other than expert witnessing?

Once you've identified your experts, the next step is the development of their opinions and the bases for them. Your objective is to help them reach their full potential as witnesses. Here is my checklist of steps to take in preparing your expert.

- ✔ Provide clear guidance about the scope of their expected testimony, including the topics you want them to prepare to testify about. Of equal importance, I was clear about areas I wished them to stay out of because of concern for potential conflicts in the opinions of other experts who were retained to render opinions on those issues. I also was concerned one of my experts might be excluded under Federal Rule of Evidence 403 on grounds of undue time consumption or cumulativeness.

- ✔ Determine materials needed for review. What documents do you have or can obtain that will assist the expert in learning about the case? Are their witnesses they might wish to interview, or statements or transcripts of witness testimony that might be of assistance. Are there site visits that would be of assistance in understanding the case or that might turn up evidence? Might a look at some accident artifacts help? Would a medical examination or review of medical records be important in forming an opinion? Are there tests that can be conducted to help form opinions? A dialog with your expert about what they might need to form their opinions and what you have available or can get to meet is most helpful. Start early with this process.

- ✔ Provide all requested materials. You want your experts to be able to answer the question: "Is there anything you needed to form your opinion that was not available or that was not provided?" with an unequivocal "no". If you hold something back from your expert once they've requested it, you potentially undermine the basis for their opinions and your credibility.

- ✔ Consider providing an opportunity for a meeting with other experts once they largely have formed their opinions. This expert "round tabling" of the case has several advantages. First, it lets you as the trial lawyer see how all the pieces fit together and to determine if there is anything missing in the story they will tell. Second, this allows the experts to know where their area of testimony will stop, and someone else's will start thus avoiding potential duplication and cumulativeness. Third, this type of discussion will provide context for their opinions and additional information about the case they might not otherwise obtain. If you view this type of meeting as unwise for any reason, however, consider as an alternative providing expert reports and disclosures of others to your experts for their review.

- ✔ Discuss orally with your experts their opinions as they develop. This will allow you to learn their thinking and the status of their work as they move through the process of forming opinions and the bases for those opinions. Discussions of this type also will allow you to guide continued development of opinions if an expert is going off track or seems stuck.

- ✔ Keep your experts advised of due dates and deadlines for reports and disclosures. Provide ample lead time for draft reports so that your team and your client will have time to review and comment upon drafts. The Federal Rules of Civil Procedure now provide that draft reports aren't discoverable[10] and communications between counsel and experts are protected, except for communications regarding compensation, facts, and assumptions.[11]

- ✔ Thoroughly prepare your experts for deposition and trial testimony. Even if they had testified many times before, go over the rules for effective testimony, stressing the need to tell the truth and to respond directly to questions that are asked. Make sure the expert is very familiar with her report or the disclosure that describes her expected testimony. If time and cost is not an issue, consider having a team member, or a partner adept at cross-examining experts and who can be prepared to examine your expert, conduct a mock cross-examination. This will give the expert a chance to "dry run" her testimony and you a chance to observe how she performs under pressure. This will also give you an opportunity to work with the expert to address deficiencies in preparation, demeanor, or approach to questions.

§ 4.06 TASK CONTROL

I touched earlier on the importance of the task list to the effective leadership and management of the litigation team. Task lists set communal expectations by telling the team what will be done, who will do it, when it will be done, and what the status of the task is.

Consider telling your team at the outset of the litigation: "If you don't own a task, don't perform the work," and "If you need help with a task, come to me and I'll find it for you." If the task isn't advancing the ball, it isn't worth doing. Suggest to the team, as the Peter Drucker quote at the beginning of this chapter implies: "Let me know when you find

---

[10] *See* Fed. R. Civ. P. 26 (b)(4)(B).

[11] *See* Fed. R. Civ. P. 26 (b)(4)(C).

tasks that really aren't worth doing. If so, we'll discuss crossing those off the task list." This avoids duplication of effort, confusion of responsibilities, unnecessary work, and avoidable expense. Stress that the team will avoid activity for activity's sake. Staying busy doing things that aren't necessary costs the client money and the team a loss of valuable resources that can be deployed in other ways.

There are a few guiding principles that will allow you and your team to decide what is worth doing and what isn't.

- ✔ Ask if the task is likely to provide information that you don't already have.
- ✔ Ask whether a legal research project is directed to finding an answer to a question that isn't obvious from the jury instructions, or that might form the basis for a motion, an objection to, or support for the admission of evidence.
- ✔ Ask whether a motion is worth bringing because it is likely to pare down the case in a meaningful way.
- ✔ Ask whether a witness's testimony needs to be gathered at all, or gathered by way of a deposition, or alternatively might be gathered by an interview or statement by the witness.
- ✔ Ask whether an expert is likely to pass muster under *Daubert* and Federal Rules of Evidence 702 and 703, whether her report and testimony is likely to make your case stronger, and whether the testimony might be duplicative of that of other experts.
- ✔ Ask whether the preparation of an exhibit for use in a motion, evidentiary hearing, or trial will be worth the time and expense associated with its preparation.

These are just a few examples, but you get the picture.

The task list also observes what was sometimes referred to in the military as the "one butt to kick" rule. I don't intend here to suggest punishment-focused management of the task list, but do intend to emphasize that the team leader should have someone to go to for each task who has authority to accomplish the task, can speak to the status of the task, and has assumed the duty to produce the deliverable. When multiple people are assigned to a specific task, the potential for confusion and duplication of effort is compounded. And no one owns the task.

The task list also allows the team leader to pay attention to details. Details matter in every discipline, but certainly in trial work. Strange as it may sound, if the team leader sees to the small things—the details—the big things have a way of taking care of themselves.

When assigning tasks, communicate to the team and assigned team member:

- The context of the task (the big picture, the why, and where this discrete task fits into the whole)
- The objective (what's the mission?)
- The deliverable (what is to be created, what does it looks like?)
- The suggested path forward (are there examples, resources to consult, tips, or leads on where to start?)
- The time budget (how long this should take and; when you've spent x hours on it and still aren't done, better come back to me and let's talk)[12]
- The deadline (when do you need to see a draft or initial work product, when does the client need it, and when does the court require it?)
- Review and feedback (spend the time debriefing; what went right, what went wrong, what can we do better).

The method you use to communicate with team members about task assignments likely will vary depending on the nature of the assignment, whether more than one person will be involved in the accomplishment of the task, and how much time you anticipate needing to explain what is needed. I enjoyed meeting in person with other partners, associates, and paralegals to discuss task assignments. This allowed for questions and answers to clarify what was needed. Sometimes, a brief email covering the above points with a "come see me if you have questions" is all that is required. Sometimes you might feel the need for an "all hands" team meeting (or for a subset of team members) either in person or

---

[12] People work at different speeds and with varying levels of efficiency. In Chapter 3, we discussed the need in team building to choose team members capable of meeting the needs of the client and the case. When work isn't getting done in a timely, efficient manner by a team member, it is the job of the team leader to coach and help the person to raise their level of proficiency. After coaching and help, if performance is substandard, as Plato's Weaver, you will need to remove a strand of the cloth that doesn't fit.

virtually to go over the task list, make assignments, discuss the desired deliverables, and make sure the team is on the same page about the work to be done. But whatever method you use, I suggest you be sure to have the team member(s) feed back to you what they understand they are supposed to do and when the assignment is due so there is a shared expectation.

I've also found that clients appreciate brief, regular meetings to understand the status of the case, ask questions, and make whatever decisions need to be made. These meetings also offer an opportunity for the client to meet the team and know which team members are responsible for various tasks.

[A] Prioritize Tasks

As Goethe observed: "Things which matter most must never be at the mercy of things which matter least."[13] All tasks are not of equal value. Front load the important stuff, the tasks that must be accomplished before something of higher priority becomes possible to address. What is important? What is urgent? What must come first before other things are possible? What really doesn't need to be done (and thus can be removed from the task list)?[14]

[B] Don't Turn Over Every Rock

I touched on this point earlier, and return to it here because it is so important. In law school examinations, we were rewarded for spotting as many issues as possible then writing about them. In complex litigation, the carry-over tendency from law school is spotting all the proverbial "rocks" that might have something lying under them, then turning them over to see what might be there. In your mind's eye, thc terrain might look something like this.

[13] Johann Wolfgang von Goethe, a polymath and writer who lived and wrote in the late 18th and early 19th centuries, was famous for his aphorisms. This quotation is among his better known.

[14] Covey, *supra*.

FIGURE 4-9

Satisfying as it might be for a diligent lawyer to want to work the field of rocks to make sure nothing is missed; this is an extraordinarily expensive process for the client and can be a distraction from the main issues in the case. For both reasons, this is a wasteful practice. Pick your spots with the overall case strategy firmly in mind. In consultation with the client, decide which of the proverbial rocks might be concealing something of value to the case, then focus on those leaving the rest lie. There are, of course, risks in not turning over all the rocks. You may indeed miss something. But you will minimize that risk with a cost/benefit analysis that weighs the expense associated with the effort against the potential benefit to be realized.

§ 4.07 CASE COST CONTROL

Effective control of the tasks to be accomplished also has a direct impact on litigation cost control.[15] You must control what is to be done and how much time is spent accomplishing it to manage costs.

---

[15] Litigation costs, used in this context, means the price of the resources employed in doing the work times the quantity of hours spent in accomplishing the work in a traditional hourly rate model.

Litigation cost drivers are easily understood but sometimes difficult to control:

- Number of tasks (complexity)
- Number of hours per task (execution efficiency)
- Hourly rate (resource cost).

Cost control requires the leader to make trade-offs among tasks, efficiency, and resource price. The simple way of thinking about litigation economics (and I admit I'm at risk here of over-simplifying) is that the cost to the client ("C") is equal to the price of each resource ("P") times the quantity of each resource used ("Q"). With this basic equation in mind, the steps that can be taken to aid in cost control for the client become obvious.

[A] Push Work to the Low-Cost Provider

This isn't necessarily the team member with the lowest billing rate. Sometimes, ten minutes of a senior partner's time who has the experience necessary to provide the answer or point the inquiry in the right direction (even with a high billing rate) will be less expensive than an hour of a more junior lawyer's time (at a lower billing rate). In fact, clients often complain that they do not get enough of the senior partner's time on their case. Likewise, a paralegal with knowledge of the documents and discovery may be able to lay her fingers on the information requested faster than more senior members of the team.

This doesn't mean that you will sacrifice quality in doing so. Astronaut John Glenn reflected on the tradeoff between cost and quality on his space flights: "It's a very sobering feeling to be *up* in space and realize one's safety factor was determined by the *lowest bidder* on a government contract." The client should not have the same concern John Glenn expressed. You aren't choosing the cheapest alternative; you are using the most cost-effective resource given the nature of the task.

Most firms still bill for their services on an hourly rate basis, and value their legal services accordingly. Clients value legal services by quality of work product, speed, user-friendliness, cost, and results. A client's perception of value is shaped in part by the cost of the services and in part by the result you obtain. Allocation of time to priority tasks in a way that controls cost while achieving the team's mission is crucial to the delivery of value-added services.

[B] Staff Leanly

An inscription on a bronze statue of a Texas Ranger that used to hold a prominent place in the lobby of Dallas Love Field read: "One riot, one Ranger." Here's the back story and the reason that inscription carried a message for those who manage litigation teams.

In the late 1800's, Captain Bill McDonald of the Texas Rangers was called to El Paso by the city fathers to prevent an illegal boxing match between two fellows named Fitzsimmons and Maher. They feared a riot would ensue. One of the sponsors of the bout was Judge Roy Bean.

Captain McDonald got on a train and went to El Paso to break up the match, as requested. The mayor met the train, expecting a large group of Rangers to help quell the expected riot. When only Captain McDonald stepped down from the train, the mayor asked where the rest of the Rangers were. Legend has it that Captain McDonald responded: "Hell! Ain't I enough? There's only one prize-fight!"[16] One riot, one Ranger.

When your case comes to trial, you don't need to outnumber the other side to win. Good choices for who the trial team members are and thorough advance preparation before you walk through the courtroom door is much more important than the number of people on your team.

Several years ago, a friend of mine and I were trying two cases in adjacent courtrooms in a federal courthouse. His case was a white-collar criminal prosecution against a single defendant who was alleged to have conspired with others to defraud investors. He was trying the case with the help of his paralegal to manage the trial exhibits. My case was a civil False Claims Act claim involving alleged violations of government accounting standards in the performance of government contracts. I was trying the case with a partner who was an expert in government contract law and a paralegal.

Our two cases had in common the approach of the government to the staffing of the trial. At a break, he invited me over to the courtroom where his case was being tried to see the forces arrayed against his client: several FBI agents, a government accountant, several lawyers, and a

[16] Actually, it is a legend. A team of Rangers showed up in El Paso causing Judge Bean to move the fight across the Rio Grande into Mexico. But it makes a good story and illustrates an important point.

couple of paralegals. I invited him over to our courtroom for a similar view: two lawyers from the Department of Justice in Washington, two lawyers from the United States Attorney's Office for the district, a lawyer for the Relator, a couple of FBI agents, a government accountant, and a paralegal. We stepped out in the hall, and he said with a wide smile, channeling General Creighton Abrams' famous line from the Battle of the Bulge: "They have us surrounded again, the poor bastards." The cases both turned out well for our clients, but this experience and others from my practice have convinced me that you are better off with the judge and jury by giving the appearance you are the party that is outnumbered. This is not a knock on government lawyers; private lawyers are equally capable of overstaffing a matter and a trial.

The message is simple: Don't task a group to do what one person can accomplish. Match the team to the anticipated workload. Staff your case with people you know can and will do the job. Avoid the entourage approach to hearings, depositions, and trials. Judges roll their eyes when a group of lawyers show up for hearings and motions, and most sit quietly taking notes while the senior partner makes the appearance. Hold down the "quantity" in the equation, to the extent prudent, to hold down the cost.

[C] Eliminate Bottlenecks

Bottlenecks in work processes occur when a single person is responsible for the creation or review of work product or the conduct of discovery, but simply doesn't have the ability to accomplish the task in a timely manner. Workflow slows and stops at the point of the bottleneck. Bottlenecks in management processes come from limitations in data sharing and decision-making bandwidth. This concept is referred to as Liebig's Law of the Minimum.[17] The principle can be visualized in this way.

[17] Liebig's law states that a chain of processes is limited in its capacity not by the total resources available, but by the scarcest resource. The capacity of the whole chain is determined by the weakest link. This illustration is referred to as Dobenecks' barrel. The shortest slat in the barrel determines the quantity of water the entire barrel can handle. Likewise, with litigation teams the smooth flow of work is limited by the ability of any one team member to do their part in the process.

FIGURE 4-10

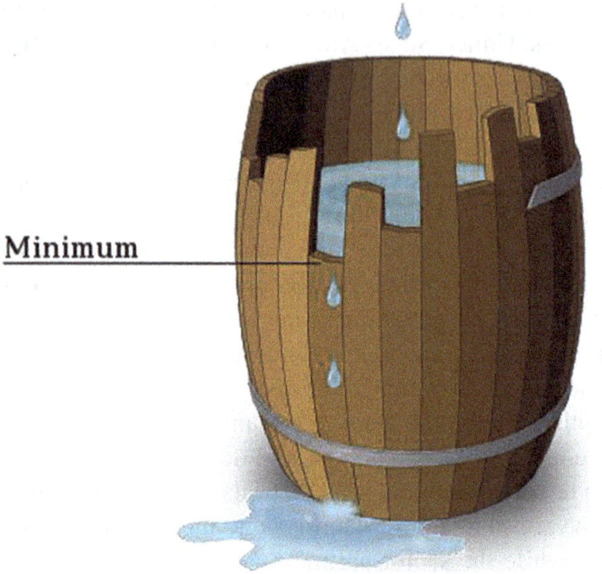

To avoid bottlenecks, I suggest you organize information for team use so that it is readily accessible. Shared information is enabling. If a team member has spent time on a project, ensure the fruits of their effort are made available to others on the team and to the client.

I tried to remind my teammates of deadlines and the importance of starting with enough lead time so that team leaders and client representatives have sufficient time to review and approve of work product, particularly pleadings and briefs that were to be submitted to the court. And most importantly, delegate authority to make decisions and perform tasks so that you, as the manager of the case, don't become the bottleneck.

[D] Maintain Team Continuity

I emphasized in Chapter 3 the importance of choosing your team members with care. Once you've on boarded them for the litigation, spent time bringing them up to speed on the facts of the client's case, assigned them tasks to accomplish, and invested in their careers by making them better at what they do, you will want to hold on to them. Spend the time to introduce your team to the client so that they will know who is professionally and personally invested in their case. Keep your team members engaged on the case and motivated to do their best for the client.

Turnover is "brain drain" and disrupts the team's flow. And clients hate turnover on your team. A new team member means repeating training with the additional investment, lost time, and increased cost that entails. Team continuity yields efficiencies and increases client satisfaction.

There is a tension, however, between continuity in your team that is good for the client and case, and monopolization of the time of other partners and associates that limit their opportunities to accept work from others and gain experience on other cases. Too much of the former and not enough sharing with others within the firm is harmful to morale and professional growth. For this reason, staffing decisions on major pieces of litigation should be candidly discussed with the client and the partnership to achieve buy in on the plan and alignment on the use of resources.

Let's turn next to the difficult problem of how to manage litigation decision-making processes to make sound decisions while avoiding pitfalls in the way humans think about problems.

CHAPTER 5
LITIGATION DECISION MAKING

"Reality is a cloud of possibilities, not a point."

—Amos Tversky

This chapter suggests methods to promote sound group decision making and seeks to attune litigators to potential pitfalls in the way they make decisions that can cause blunders and damage client relationships. Much can be said on the topic of human decision-making processes, some of which I discussed in Chapter 1. Semester-long courses are taught on the subject. Numerous books have been written on the art of effective decision making. Behavioral psychologist Daniel Kahneman won a Nobel Memorial Prize in Economics in 2002 for his work with Amos Tversky[1] describing how the mind works when set to the task of deciding something. Behavioral economist Richard Thaler, who collaborated with Drs. Kahneman and Tversky early in his career, won the Nobel Prize in 2017 for incorporating psychologically more realistic assumptions, or at least assumptions that lead to good predictions, into the analysis of economic decision making. Decision making in complex litigation, of course, is grounded in the economics of the case.

In civil litigation, the typical remedy is money damages. In criminal litigation, fines may be imposed in addition to a loss of liberty. In both cases, lawyers representing the parties to the litigation must be paid, either by the litigants in civil cases or the public in criminal cases. These economic costs are important considerations in litigation decision making.

Let's turn first to common decision-making paths, next to effective organization of the decision-making process, and then to myths about how decisions are made. We then can turn to mental traps—common biases, heuristics, and fallacies—that prevent good decision making and that we must overcome as litigation team leaders.

---

[1] Amos Tversky, who was Daniel Kahneman's research partner and friend, died in 1996. He did not share in the Nobel Prize for their research because the prize is not given posthumously. Dr. Kahneman passed away in 2024.

§ 5.01 DECISION-MAKING PATHS

Perhaps the best way of thinking about how humans decide is the System 1 and System 2 model proposed by Daniel Kahneman and Amos Tversky. In his book *Thinking, Fast and Slow,* Dr. Kahneman describes a number of cognitive errors and biases that undermine the quality of our judgments. The book is a master work summarizing extensive research in the field of behavioral psychology.[2]

Dr. Kahneman describes two metaphorical actors: System 1 who is fast and intuitive and System 2 who is slow and analytical. Both actors are at play in litigation decision making. The System 1 thinker is automatic, intuitive, instinctive, primary, rapid, and largely blind to information that is not right in front of him. This is the "fast on your feet" mode of thought. Think objections at trial, or follow up in cross-examination. The System 2 thinker is considered, effortful, focused, secondary, slower, and lazy (in the sense of slow to seek alternate paths). This is the "methodical" mode of thought. Think preparation of client evaluation letters, discovery requests, motions, and outlines for opening statements, witness examinations, and closing arguments.

Lawyers like to think that they live in a world of reason and careful deliberation—a System 2 environment—and that judges and clients live in that world as well. They don't. Reflexive thinking is the easier path; deliberate thinking is hard work. Both can lead to errors. We entertain myths about how we decide important questions in litigation as intelligent, rational, analytical lawyers. And we're frequently wrong.

§ 5.02 GROUP DECISION-MAKING CHALLENGES

The objective of any decision-making process is to arrive efficiently at a conclusion that takes input from those best positioned to give an informed view on an issue and incorporates their best thinking. Whether the decision to be made is a relatively small one, a "may I come by your office with a quick question" type, or a major one that involves the preparation of a briefing paper and PowerPoint® and is an "all hands on deck" type, the *result* likely will be suboptimal if the *process* is poor. The first

[2] Kahneman, *supra*. If you read just one book about how humans make decisions, I think this is the one to spend your time on.

step, then, is to create an atmosphere conducive to good decision making. I suggest you focus on four key points in designing a sound process.

[A] Composition

Who should be involved? Client input is crucial on any number of issues that may arise during complex litigation, but may not always be needed. As we discussed in Chapter 1 when setting client communication patterns, you and your team need to understand when client input is required on decisions, and when it is not.

I found that forming a small group to think through an issue and arrive at a solution could be done quickly—for example, the associate doing the research and writing and the paralegal gathering the supporting documents. On other occasions, days would be spent preparing for a client board meeting to brief the directors on the status of the litigation and make important strategic decisions. The key is to ask who might have helpful input on the issue and should be consulted, and whether that input should be aired with others at the same time in a meeting or can be obtained in a series of separate exchanges with others by the person or group who will make the decision.

[B] Context

What is the environment for the decision process? Setting the right environment for good decision making requires some thought about where you can have a candid conversation with the right materials available for the participants. The range of circumstances that can work for you as a team leader is practically endless.

On one extreme, I've participated in many whispered discussions with my client and co-counsel in a courthouse hallway about how to proceed with a witness, how to respond to a judge's question, or whether to accept a settlement demand. The only materials I typically had available or needed were those in my trial notebook. On the other extreme, I've hosted multi-day off site meetings where local counsel in various cases around the country traveled to attend discussions about the status of their cases, the development of experts, and rulings in other cases, as well as to discuss strategy for the family of cases. These meetings were supported by detailed agendas, notebooks of materials relevant to the intended discussion, and PowerPoint® presentations. You must build the appropriate environment to support the type of decision you need to make, and the urgency of that decision.

[C] Communication

What are the means of dialog among the participants? In my opinion, the best are conducted face-to-face. Among the many good reasons for favoring this method of communication is the ability to "read the room," to ask questions and follow-up, and to build camaraderie and investment in the decision. But team members often are spread across the United States, if not the world, may not be operating on the same workday as other team members, may be working remotely a good part of the time, and may be living most of their professional lives on telephone or Zoom® conference calls. A face-to-face meeting may not be possible or necessary. Of course, however the conversation is arranged, you should give due consideration to the protection of client confidences.

[D] Control

How will you control the process and content of the decision to reach a desirable result? Typically, as leader, you should guide the discussion. If time permits and the situation calls for it, an agenda listing the issues to be discussed, the person responsible for the agenda item, and the time allotted to a discussion of that issue is helpful in guiding the dialog. I've found that discussions were more fruitful and efficient when I, or another team member, began a decision process with a statement of the question to be decided followed by a brief background on the issue. As with any active listening process, before reaching the point where a decision is announced, summarize what you think you've heard to make sure the participants are aligned in their understanding. A clear statement of the decision that is reached, together with the designation of the person or persons to carry out the decision and the time frame in which those actions are to be made, should conclude the discussion.

These four considerations are common sense for experienced team leaders and likely come as second nature to you. But giving some thought to these points is likely to improve whatever process you adopt and thus improve the decision itself. There are several specific challenges inherent in group decision-making processes, however, that deserve separate comment and a suggested prescription for addressing these challenges.

[E] Making Sense of Ambiguous Situations

We already touched briefly on the importance of a shared understanding of the situation. This means orienting the group to what is known about the issue under discussion and what question needs to be resolved. Participants in complex litigation processes are subject to the "fog of war" that obscures the "battlefield." Factual understanding may be incomplete. Uncertainty about what law will be applied may leave open questions about the legal structure of the dispute. All of this is to say that you should try to couch the decision-making process in light of the objectives set by the client—your North Star—so that your team doesn't lose sight of the goal even when the factual details are unclear.

A good example of this came during a settlement conference in one case among several involving a series of helicopter accidents. My client stated: "We need to try this case to prevent future suits of the same kind." The objective and the strategy made sense, but the ambiguity was in the term "of the same kind." Did all of the pending suits have the same factual and legal features? The case we were discussing was one of those rare "black swan events" that had little to do with the other cases we were litigating—no product design or manufacturing issues. When we made sense of this ambiguity, as best we could, it became apparent an inexpensive settlement rather than a week's long jury trial made sense.

℞ – Ask: Do I understand the context of the decision to be made? Am I imposing my framing of the question on others, and is it a fair way of characterizing the issue? What does success look like for the client?

[F] Avoiding Process Loss

Group wisdom comes when decisions reflect the thinking of the most knowledgeable. We want our decision processes to take full advantage of everyone's thinking, and our ultimate decision to benefit from the input of those with the most relevant knowledge. The goal is to have the group's decision reflect the best thinking of all members of the team. That may not always be the most senior or experienced lawyer in the room. Who did the research, the document mining, the analysis and is able to comment knowledgeably? This isn't necessarily the oldest, the most experienced, or the team leader. And it isn't necessarily the person who takes up the most "airtime" in the discussion.

I recall sitting in a particularly animated conversation with opposing counsel in a chambers conference during a trial to obtain a ruling on the admissibility of proposed testimony by a witness. (Yes, adversarial hearings are a form of group decision making, with the person in the black robe playing the role of the person President George W. Bush described as "the decider.") As counsel described what he thought the witness would say, I looked over at my associate, who was slowly shaking his head. I asked him whether he agreed with the opponent's counsel. He said: "I know that's not what the witness said, but everyone else seems to have heard it differently. Here's what the deposition transcript says." If he'd sat quietly through the discussion, we would not have had the benefit of his insight into the expected trial testimony of the witness based on earlier deposition testimony, and the ruling likely would have been different.

℞ – Ask: Are all perspectives represented and expressed? Are the lawyers and clients interacting, and acting independently? Is everyone with information bearing on the issue speaking up and engaging?

[G] Avoiding Decision Fatigue

This phrase is a fancy, psychology-speak way of saying that as we get tired or face many decisions simultaneously, our ability to make good decisions diminishes. Humans have different capacities for work and varying abilities to maintain concentration and focus on a task. But all of us have experienced the phenomenon that the quality of our decision making deteriorates after long sessions. We need to recognize when this begins to happen, and take a break or call a halt.

In circumstances where you control the pace and timing of the decision making, it is perfectly acceptable to conclude a meeting to let everyone "sleep on" the possible decision. In situations where you aren't in control, but feel the quality of the decisions is affected by distraction or fatigue, you can say so and ask for a break.

In a long trial with a judge who was feeling decidedly under the weather, I began to notice that as our trial day went on, the judge's rulings seemed more random and less favorable. My co-counsel observed the same thing. At a break, we suggested that because we were making good progress on our trial schedule, were between witnesses, and everyone had been working hard, taking the rest of the day off might make good sense. The judge seemed relieved at the suggestion and agreed. The recess served to break the decision fatigue cycle.

℞ – Are there ways of limiting the number of decisions we/our client/ the judge needs to make? Is this a good time to stop for the day?

[H] Avoiding "Groupthink"

This phrase is attributed to psychologist Irving Janis.[3] This is a mode of thinking people engage in when they are deeply involved in a cohesive in-group. The members' striving for unanimity overrides their motivation to realistically consider alternative courses of action resulting in missteps in decision making. We need to watch for feelings of invulnerability, rationalizing away disconfirming data, or discounting warnings. We must strive to stimulate constructive conflict in the mode of an argument among friends. The process should look more like a hockey game with smooth contact than a golf match with polite quietness.

Examples of this phenomenon abound, but a common example might illustrate the concept. Juries can fall victim to groupthink. Jurors might change their own opinions for the sake of group cohesion. Some members may also do this because they want to seem like a team player, others because they tire of the deliberations and want to go about their lives. The 1957 movie "12 Angry Men" is a good illustration of the "groupthink" effect. A fictional jury deliberating the guilt of a young man charged with killing his abusive father begins with a near unanimous verdict of guilty. But the votes in favor of acquittal grow as further discussion and deliberation ensues over whether there is reasonable doubt the young man did it.

℞ – Ask: Are there large power gradients in the group? Is there vigorous debate? Is my group too homogeneous? Are we open to possible alternatives?

Remember, to meet group decision-making challenges we must:

- Clearly frame the issue to be decided,
- Include those with necessary information about the issue to be decided, and
- Stay attuned to the internal dynamics of the team to make sure all voices and perspectives are heard so that the thinking of the most knowledgeable arises.

---

[3] Irving Janis, *Groupthink* (1982).

§ 5.03 DECISION-MAKING MYTHS

Let's next address some myths that should be debunked.[4]

[A] Myth #1—"*We are perfectly rational actors.*"

Economists hypothesize a rational decision maker that seeks a perfect market solution to optimize gain—the utility maximizer or *Homo Economicus*. In reality, we substitute "satisficing"—a solution good enough for the time and purpose—for optimizing. *Homo Sapiens* search for alternatives only until we find acceptable solutions.[5]

What does this mean in practice? If we accept that humans aren't always rational actors, we must accept a certain randomness, short-sighted self-interest, or even whim that creeps into the way litigants, opposing counsel, and the court might make decisions. I don't have enough fingers and toes to count the number of times, for example, that I've explained to a client the possibility that though a particular motion is well-taken and should be granted, there is a random chance of an adverse result—a result unrelated to the merits of the motion but the result of the judge's foibles.

[B] Myth #2—"*We use data and analytical rigor in our decision making.*"

No, not always. We use heuristics—rules of thumb—which are known mental sets that substitute for and offer easier solutions than doing the hard work of analyzing a problem in a deliberate, System 2 way.[6] Shortcuts save us time and effort and frequently lead to acceptable, albeit less than perfect, results.

We use the System 1 way of thinking to compare the problem before us with a problem we confronted and solved in the past through pattern recognition. If System 1 doesn't readily find an answer to a question, it automatically finds a related question that has an easier answer. If

[4] For those interested in digging deeper into the art of decision making, there are two programs available through *The Great Courses* company. *See* Michael A. Roberto, *The Art of Critical Decision Making*, and Ryan Hamilton, *Human Decision Making*.

[5] *See* Richard H. Thaler, *From Homo Economicus to Homo Sapiens*, 14(1) J. Econ. Perspect. 133–14 (2000).

[6] Kahneman, *supra* at 98; ("a simple procedure that helps find adequate, though often imperfect, answers to difficult questions.")

there is a close enough fit, we adopt the earlier solution without starting from scratch, sorting through the applicable data and thinking through a resolution perfectly fitted to the problem.

We may answer an easier question framed in one's own mind without realizing the substitution.[7] This is part of our "mental shotgun"—our imprecise control in targeting a response to a specific question that might prove hard to answer. Or we sometimes do so intentionally.

This frequently plays out in in courtrooms during oral argument. A judge might ask a lawyer a question about how the holding in a specific case affects the issue before the court, and receive an answer about a holding in a case the lawyer is more familiar with or that better supports his position. The response addresses a question that wasn't asked but that was easier to answer. In trial lawyer speak, the answer is objectionable on the grounds it is non-responsive.

A client might ask what the chances are we will win summary judgment, and I might answer that in my experience courts grant summary judgments only 20% of the time, and then may be susceptible to reversal on appeal. The client's question addressed the case at hand. The answer I substituted offered typical odds of victory on summary judgment—a question that is easier to answer.

When you need data and rigorous analysis in decision making, you need discipline to resort to the harder work of System 2 thinking, but this doesn't happen automatically.

[C] Myth #3—"*We do not let emotions guide our decisions.*"

We not only think, but we feel. The two are difficult to separate. Good decisions are high in both IQ, the standard measure of reasoning ability, and EQ, the ability to understand and manage emotions. As we discussed in Chapter 2, the human brain is wired so that our centers of cognition and emotion are tied together.[8] They don't operate entirely independently.

There's nothing wrong with acknowledging that our decision making has an emotional aspect to it. This is where our sense of joy comes from when justice is done, outrage boils up when it is denied, commitment is born when our clients need us, and passion develops for our profession and what we do. The trick is to recognize what aspect of

[7] *Id.* at 97–99.

[8] Rolls, *supra* at 224.

our thought processes guide us when making decisions, and to balance them appropriately.

[D] Myth #4—"*Blunders are committed only by the unintelligent and incapable.*"

Smart people can make bad choices. We're all human and therefore imperfect. We sometimes lack the time, discipline, and energy to do the hard analytical work to avoid mistakes. While I would bet on intelligent, capable people to arrive at sound decisions more consistently, they too commit errors in judgment.

As Dr. Kahneman notes, even in the absence of time pressures in our decision making, maintaining a coherent train of thought requires discipline. We have a limited "budget of effort" to work with.[9] And this leaves us vulnerable to a lack of will power and patience that can lead to poor decision making, no matter how smart we are.

The leadership and management of complex cases imposes enormous pressure on you to deliver for the client. Long days and nights of work are physically wearing. Time pressures imposed by the court and client limit the ability to slow down and think through issues, and are emotionally draining. The sheer scope of factual and legal issues in high stakes litigation and the need to master the facts and law are mentally draining. Little wonder, then, that our "budget of effort" can be exhausted, leading even smart, talented lawyers to commit judgment errors.

[E] Myth #5—"*The team leader decides.*"

Decision making is a product of the simultaneous activity of people at multiple levels of the litigation team. High stakes decisions are a product of complex social, emotional, and political processes. Even in very hierarchical teams, the leader must depend upon the client and team members for their input on the facts and law when making decisions.

In my view, the best decisions arise from group decision-making processes where the team leader involves others who have relevant knowledge and perspective on the issue to be decided, actively solicits their input, and weighs what they have to say. While you must, in

[9] *Id.* at 40–43 ("the lazy controller").

consultation with the client, make the final call as "the decider," the decision will be the product of input from others as well. Those contributing to the final decision might be the associate who performed the legal research, the paralegal who located and assembled the relevant documents, the jury consultant who analyzed the results of a mock trial, the expert who explained the underlying science and its implications for the client's case, or in-house counsel who provides perspective on the aims of the client. The team leader in consultation with the client will make the call. But the team will provide the grist for the decision-making mill.

[F] Myth #6—"*Decision follows analysis and action follows decision.*"

Decision making often unfolds in a non-linear fashion with solutions arising before the problem is completely identified. Decisions often evolve over time in an iterative process. We do something, see if it works, and then do something else to see if that works better. This cycle of problem definition, action, and assessment may not conform with the common perception of decision making as a linear process, but this is how the real world works most of the time.

This iterative process is at the core of decision making under conditions of uncertainty. We attempt to incrementally improve the shaping of our decisions by looking back to previous events to harvest whatever learning they hold, update them with new information, and apply that perspective to our current circumstance. This process is the essence of the scientific method, and is incapsulated mathematically in Bayes' Theorem[10] and philosophically in Process Philosophy concepts.[11] Most decisions we face in complex litigation involve judgment calls we must

---

[10] For a description of Thomas Bayes's theorem and its implications for reasoning toward solutions to problems *see* Sharon Bertsch McGrayne, *The Theory That Would Not Die* (2011). Simply stated, the theorem sets out a method for getting smarter by continuously updating with new facts and perspectives what we think we know. The resulting improved perspective then becomes the new base case as the process repeats.

[11] The father of Process Philosophy is Alfred North Whitehead, famous mathematician, physicist, and philosopher. His *magnum opus* on Process Philosophy is *Process and Reality* (1929). For a good summary of basic concepts of Process Philosophy, *see* John B. Cobb, Jr. & David Ray Griffin, *Process Theology—an Introductory Exposition* 13–28 (1976). In Process Philosophy, the present and the decisions we make in the present are influenced by the past and what we think we already know, and will influence the future course of events.

make without a perfect understanding of the facts or the consequences of the alternatives we might choose. Our best path to a decision, however, is to follow this logical flow, repeating the process as necessary as we "work the problem" we face.

This process has made sense to me for a long time. During Basic Cadet Training at the Air Force Academy, our class spent time on the Confidence Course[12] taking turns leading each other in overcoming challenges designed to test our creativity and leadership abilities. The challenges were for the most part heavily physical, for example getting the team over a high wall with a few ropes in a limited time. The best solutions arose when the Cadet designated as the leader for a particular obstacle took input from the team about alternative solutions, settled on a plan, announced it, and began to implement it. But as the exercise unfolded, the effective leaders were open to changing the plan if things weren't working or if someone came up with an alternative that offered the potential for a better outcome. Frequently, the plan the leader initially adopted wasn't the plan that got us over the wall. Adaptation of the plan based on new inputs frequently carried the day. I've observed this same phenomenon in litigation teams as well.

§ 5.04 DECISION-MAKING TRAPS

We can now turn to several mental traps common to litigation decision making. We are subject to many cognitive biases and fallacies—systematic mistakes in thinking based on how we are "hardwired" as humans.[13] I focus here on a specific subset of these mistakes—ten in number—that are prevalent in complex litigation and that seem to have an outsized effect on the outcome of cases. Let's discuss how to spot them, and a prescription for how to avoid them.

---

[12] A Confidence Course consists of a series of obstacles that are designed to challenge the participants' physical abilities, teamwork, and problem-solving skills and help build their confidence as leaders.

[13] Dr. Kahneman's *Thinking, Fast and Slow* provides a lengthy list of tricks the human mind can play on us as we make decisions. Others who have studied and written about decision making supplement and expand the list.

[A] #1—Sunk Cost Fallacy

This well-known effect results from an over-commitment to past investments and prior decisions.[14] We fall into this fallacy when we abandon incremental thinking and ignore the return on the next dollar invested. Effort already expended and dollars already spent should not form the basis for future decisions. Instead, the focus should be on returns from the next investment in time, resources, and money. Examples of this fallacy at play in litigation jump readily to mind. Here are a few I've observed in my own practice.

- A client says: "We've already spent $1M on this case; we must recoup our investment." Well, no. Those dollars are out the door and gone forever. The question is whether the next dollars spent on the case are likely to improve the client's position in the litigation. If not, stop spending money on the matter.
- An insurer invests $5 million in fees and costs chasing a possible, small opportunity to save $5 to $10 million off a policy with a $100 million limit. Without considering the probabilities of success in the case, it seems obvious one would not spend $5 million to "save" $5 million. Sure, there are circumstances where clients litigate on principle, but insurers usually don't fall into that class of litigants.
- An insurer invests $1.5 million in the prosecution of a subrogation action to attempt to recover $1.4 million plus interest on a hull loss claim—the amount paid to the insured for the loss of the airplane. Even if the insurer had won at trial, it doesn't make sense to spend in fees and costs what you might recover in principal and interest. Adding insult to injury, the insurer lost the claim.

℞ – Ask: What are the costs, both monetary and strategic, of the next action we will take? What are the benefits? At what point does it become clear that further expenditures of time, effort, and money are unlikely to accomplish the goal? Sometimes, it is helpful to ask whether you would take the proposed steps if you were just starting the case and writing on a clean slate.

---

[14] David Ronayne, Daniel Sgiori, & Anthony Tuckwell, *How Susceptible Are You to the Sunk Cost Fallacy?*, Harv. Bus. Rev. (July 15, 2021).

When you focus on the next dollar to be spent, understanding that past dollars spent are gone, you engage in sound incremental thinking. If you conclude that further expenditures are unlikely to move the client toward the goal, it is time to have a candid conversation with the client about that reality. Tell your client not to throw good money after bad. Your client likely will be disappointed about the money they spent, but will appreciate avoiding additional unnecessary expense.

[B] #2—Framing Effect

Frames are mental models, sometimes called paradigms,[15] that we use to understand the world. How the question is asked and what assumptions are made may determine the answer we give. Different ways of presenting or receiving the same information often evoke different emotions in the recipient of the information.[16]

If I tell my client they have a better than even chance of winning at trial (expressed statistically, let's say, as 60%), this statement would be more reassuring than saying we would lose a little less than half the time (say about 40%). The data are the same, but the perception is different. How you express information as a team leader—how you frame the issue—has an impact. Further, framing questions as opportunities causes us to be more cautious, and framing a question as a loss causes us to accept more risk.[17] Here are a few examples to illustrate this effect.

- A jury verdict awarding $200 million in damages in a patent case is a description of the outcome of a trial. If the client takes that fact and frames it negatively, they might say: "We asked for $1 billion in damages, but we only got $200 million so we lost." The two statements, though describing the same result, *mean different things* because they evoke different reactions.[18]
- If I am told I require surgery that features a survival rate of 90%, I might react positively and with hope. If the surgeon

[15] *See* Kuhn, *supra*.

[16] Kahneman, *supra* at 88 ("framing effects").

[17] Daniel Kahneman & Amos Tversky, *Choices, Values, and Frames*, 34 Am. Psychol. (1984).

[18] Kahneman, *supra* at 363–64.

presents the same information in a negative frame, saying the mortality rate is 10%, I likely will react with greater concern.[19]

℞ – Ask: Are we framing the question as a win or a loss? What other frames should we adopt? What are our assumptions, and are they right?

Legal problem solving usually has a template in the law—causes of action and elements, legally cognizable defenses, statutory language or definitions, standards of proof or review. Use them as a framework for decision that lays out the facts in as neutral a fashion as possible. Offer alternative frames to contextualize the information.

[C] #3—Anchoring Effect

An initial reference point can distort perceptions. A person asked to consider a specific number as a possible solution to an estimation problem subconsciously allows that number to induce an answer closer to that number.[20] The data supplied with the possible solution in effect *anchors* the estimation process and replaces a potential estimate that might have been offered in the absence of the anchor. The initial reference doesn't have to be logically related to create an anchor. We subconsciously begin at the reference point and adjust from there, even when the reference point is arbitrary or groundless.

The anchoring effect has been studied extensively by behavioral scientists and is actively used by parties in litigation. Consider these examples.

- Drs. Tversky and Kahneman conducted a study where they rigged a wheel of fortune and asked their subject to spin it. The wheel was set up to produce either a 10 or 65. The subjects were then asked: "What percentage of United Nations membership is comprised of African nations?" The subjects then guessed an answer. For those spinning 10, the average answer was 25%. For those spinning 65, the average answer was 45%. The guessed answer was anchored with a completely irrelevant number. (The actual percentage is 28%.)[21]

---

[19] *Id.* at 367.

[20] *Id.* at 120 ("anchoring effect").

[21] *Id.* at 427.

- In settlement negotiations, the parties frequently start with offers or demands that stretch the bounds of credulity given the facts and law in their case. In doing so, they hope to locate the range of possible settlements in a way favorable to their clients. I was involved in serial product litigation for a manufacturer and participated in a mediation in a case headed to trial where a very large demand had been made. The plaintiff sought about $90 million in damage in a wrongful death case—a very high anchor. Most of the claim was based upon future lost earnings. Our economic analysis indicated the loss was less than a tenth of that. After some back and forth, it became apparent plaintiff would only "make a move downward" in the negotiations on a proportional basis to our moves upward—a losing proposition for my client. So, we walked away from the mediation and went to trial. The plaintiff ultimately got a disappointing "take nothing" verdict in that case. The strategy of a high or low anchoring demand, however, doesn't always disadvantage the party employing it.
- In closing arguments, each side might try to anchor the jury's deliberation about a damages number at the highest or lowest plausible number. A plaintiff's lawyer might suggest an award of non-economic damages calculated on a payment per day for the pain and suffering to be endured by her client (a *per diem* argument) and then invite the jury to multiply that amount by the years of life expectancy of the plaintiff to determine a verdict amount. The hope is that their number might create the starting point for juror deliberations about a possible award.

℞ – Ask: What is the relevance of the starting point? Why was that reference point chosen? Do we walk away and start over in a different frame?[22]

Settlement discussions are a bit easier to manage when the anchoring effect is at play. Sometimes, counter-anchors can be employed. Sometimes this is impossible because "$0" is the bottom and the top is virtually limitless. But it is possible to name the game and refuse to play it.

[22] Don Rushing, Linda Lane, & Erin Bosman, *Anchors Away: Attacking Dollar Suggestions for Non -Economic Damages in Closing*, Def. Couns. J. 378–85 (July 2003).

Closing arguments where an anchor is employed are more difficult to manage. It isn't possible to simply walk away and start over. It certainly is possible to offer judges and juries a different frame by tying the facts and law of the case to your own anchor. The hard fact, however, is that this reframing will still leave the jury or judge with the opponent's anchor to consider and react to. And people do react to anchors, however irrelevant to the question they are asked to answer or how persuasive you are in naming the game.

[D] #4—What You See Is All There Is

This heuristic, named WYSIATI by Drs. Kahneman and Tversky, comes into play as System 1 operates to create a coherent story based on limited evidence, relying on information fresh in the memory or most available as the basis for decision. We have a strong tendency to focus on what is in front of us at the time, and fail to realize and account for the fact that any aspect of life to which our attention is somehow directed, even if we did not ourselves intentionally direct our attention to it, will loom large in our evaluation of a situation. We fall prey to tunnel vision. We tend to judge the frequency of a type of occurrence by the ease with which instances come to the judging person's mind. As Dr. Kahneman notes: "The world in our heads is not a precise replica of reality; our expectations about the frequency of events are distorted by the prevalence and emotional intensity of the messages to which we are exposed."[23]

Data most available to us is most persuasive. And we spin stories from the available information without seeking contrary or clarifying data. We can be insensitive to the quality and quantity of the information we use to form our stories.[24] Or ignore changes that occur and that change how we might view the data. As Dr. Kahneman notes: "Nothing in life is as important as you think it is when you are thinking about it."[25]

One result is that lawyers can become overconfident in their judgments because of the coherence of their stories, even if backed by little evidence. If you don't lift your gaze and look beyond the confines of the data readily presented to you, you will miss the bigger picture. Here are a few examples to illustrate this point.

---

[23] Kahneman, *supra* at 138 ("availability heuristic").

[24] *Id.* at 85–87.

[25] *Id.* at 402 ("the focusing illusion").

- For many years aviation lawyers defending actions brought in U.S. courts arising out of foreign accidents strongly believed that they would always win *forum non conveniens* dismissal motions in favor of a foreign forum, or change of venue motions to more favorable jurisdictions. The evidence before them was a string of victories dating back many years. Then a change in a corporate headquarters of an aircraft manufacturer, and state court filings in Chicago that no longer were removable to federal court on diversity of citizenship grounds or transfer motions for improper venue began to change that story. The Illinois state courts frequently declined to dismiss or transfer the cases brought in their jurisdiction.
- We are exposed to a 24-hour, seven day per week news feed reporting criminal activity. One watching this coverage might conclude that our society is getting less safe and more violent. That is the data that presents itself to our System 1 thinking and forms the basis for a narrative that our country is experiencing an increase in crime. Yet the data says our American society is becoming less violent over time.[26]
- A turkey raised on a farm might feel life is very good. He is fed by the farmer, put away in a safe place at night out of reach of predators, and comfortable in the company of his fellow turkeys. Then Thanksgiving comes.

℞ – Ask: What information are we relying on? How reliable is it? What other information is out there to access? What might that tell us about the situation?

I suggest you try to put the issue for decision in the broadest reasonable context. Seek out data that will contextualize and inform your decision but that might not be easily available.

[E] #5—Overconfidence Bias

This is also known as the optimism bias or planning fallacy.[27] We fall prey to this bias when we look at the world through rose-colored glasses. I think of this as "The Lake Wobegon Effect." Garrison

---

[26] Steven Pinker, *The Better Angels of Our Nature* (2012).

[27] Kahneman, *supra* at 25053.

Keillor's famous monologues from the long running "Prairie Home Companion" radio show were entitled "The News from Lake Wobegon" "where all the women are strong, all the men good looking, and all the children above average."[28] Our over-optimism might be based on past favorable outcomes. This bias can invade our forecasting by making us more confident of what we think can happen, how quickly things can be accomplished, how little things will cost, and what work can be avoided. Or simply on our own belief that we are better forecasters than we really are. Examples in life and litigation abound.

- John Krakauer wrote about a May 1996 Everest ascent when five people died high on the mountain in the death zone because they failed to turn back before weather turned bad and night fell. The guides for the ascent felt they had the peak within their reach, were buoyed by their success in past climbs, and continued toward the peak when it was time to turn back. As Krakauer cautioned in his book *Up Into Thin Air*:[29] "Avoid the clinically delusional."
- With the passage of Proposition 1A in 2008, California began to build a high-speed rail link between San Francisco and Anaheim estimated to cost $33 billion. By 2024, the estimate was $128 billion and growing, and the rail link was not operating.
- I've seen good trial lawyers proclaim: "We've won this type of case the last three times we've tried it; this one will be no different." But if the facts are different and not as favorable, or if the jury panel is comprised of people who are not as accepting of your story as previous panels, the result very well might be different. A lawyer tried a breach of contract case to a jury and received a favorable verdict. But there was a counterclaim on which the jury deadlocked. The judge declared a mistrial as to the entire case, and it had to be retried. A few months later, a different jury hearing the same case, same lawyers, and same witnesses found against the client on the contract case and awarded compensatory and punitive damages on the tort counts in the counterclaim, an unhappy surprise.

---

[28] Garrison Keillor, *The Keillor Reader* (2014).
[29] John Krakauer, *Up Into Thin Air* (1997).

℞ – Ask: What could go wrong, and what will be the cost? Consider a "red team"—someone outside the situation—to ask hard questions.

We need to temper our forecasting with hard data—prior history, similar cases, and so forth. We need to sensitize our forecasting with alternative outcomes. The use of mock juries and focus groups to caution our optimism plays a helpful role in avoiding this bias.

[F] #6—Loss Aversion

This is the tendency to feel the pain of a loss more than we feel the pleasure of a gain.[30] For this reason, we tend to respond more strongly to potential losses than to potential gains.[31] We also tend in our mental accounting to assess risks in isolation rather than by putting them in a broader context.[32] In part, this is a framing problem, but it also is a basic feature of how humans view prospects for gain and loss. When we are confronted with the potential for both loss and gain, we can weigh the two against each other and "place our bet." This is yet another reason to use tools such as decision trees to lay out for the client the risks associated with a decision. As I pointed out in Chapter 1, laying out the potential flow of a case and quantifying the expected values of various outcomes helps to frame for the client in a more neutral way the potential gains and losses in a case.

- In a lawsuit where both parties are counterclaiming against each other, each claim presents the opportunity for a loss (a disappointing verdict) or a win (a satisfactory verdict).
- The decision a plaintiff's lawyer makes in deciding to take a case on a contingent fee basis involves the knowledge that a loss means no fee, but a win might yield a handsome return on her time. In mixed gambles of this sort, loss aversion causes extremely risk-averse choices.

[30] Matthew Rabin & Richard Thaler, *Anomalies—Risk Aversion*, 15(1) J. Econ. Perspect. 226 (Winter 2001). Professors Thaler and Rabin, explain a very technical topic, risk aversion, in a very entertaining way.

[31] Kahneman, *supra* at 283–86 ("loss aversion").

[32] Thaler & Rabin, *supra* at 226.

- In situations where there are only bad choices, for example when a sure loss (an expensive settlement) is compared to the probability of a larger loss (a trial involving substantially larger exposure), "diminished sensitivity causes risk seeking."[33]

Surprising, but that's what the research shows.

℞ – Ask: What is the broader context of the risk to be considered? What are the costs and the benefits that should be taken into account? What is the expected value of the bet the client is being asked to take?

[G] #7—Confirmation Bias

This is the human tendency to gather and rely on information that confirms our existing views; to unwittingly seek data that are likely to be compatible with beliefs we already hold.[34] Believing is an automatic operation of System 1, as we try to quickly make sense of our environment. Unbelieving is an effortful operation of System 2, as we methodically analyze what we've been told.

This bias comes into play for litigators as we look for case or statutory authority to support our client's position, or testimonial or documentary evidence to provide facts to buttress our arguments. To state the obvious, we need to keep our eyes open to contrary law and evidence to overcome the confirmation bias. But this requires discipline and a choice to be a bit skeptical about what you are hearing.

A closely allied bias is the affect heuristic. A person's likes and dislikes in one area unknowingly determine the person's beliefs about other aspects of the world.[35] We let conclusions dominate over considered arguments. Assumptions about human nature—"in particular, about the choices that people may make and the consequences of their choices for themselves and for society"[36]—can cause us to miscalculate. My view of how people might make choices in particular circumstances is heavily

---

[33] *Id.* at 285.

[34] Kahneman, *supra* at 80–81 ("confirmation bias").

[35] *Id.* at 103 ("the affect heuristic").

[36] *Id.* at 141. I purposefully am conflating the concept of affect heuristics and concerns about availability, emotion, and risk as those seem allied concerns to me.

weighted by my own life experiences, and may not reflect the views of those who matter in a case. We must watch our decision making to make sure our likes and dislikes do not replace careful consideration of evidence and arguments that run contrary to our own preferences. I offer a few examples to demonstrate this cluster of biases.

- Trial lawyers sometimes fall in love with their own arguments. We search for evidence, case law, and statutes that support our position, and discount information that doesn't. We "proof text"—a method of using a portion of a text that validates our argument without regard for the context of the text. We conduct discovery to gather facts that confirm our impressions and that prove our case, but may not seek or focus on information that explains or buttresses our opponent's.
- The scientific method tests a null hypothesis by attempting to refute it. But humans seek information likely to be compatible with beliefs they already hold. The objective is confirmation instead of falsification. In the last few election cycles, for example, there is a belief among some unsuccessful candidates and their supporters that an election was stolen through voter suppression or fraud. Those holding this view often are not open at all to the argument there is no evidence to support such a claim or to contrary evidence suggesting the claim is untrue.
- I was always cautious in the use of humor in the courtroom, reserving it for situations where everyone could enjoy a laugh together without anyone feeling they were the butt of the joke. But I have a brilliant trial lawyer friend who used his rapier wit on many occasions against witnesses, opposing counsel, and even a judge or two. And he seemed to get away with it because the jury was entertained by it. The confidence I had in my view on this point was tested, but not changed, by his effective, humorous asides. He's just funnier than I am.

℞ – Ask: Who can be a contrarian to question our evidence and play "Devil's Advocate?" What would our opponent say if she were here, putting the obverse case in the best light? What evidence are we overlooking that provides a different perspective on the question, and should we credit it?

[H] #8—Narrative Fallacy

Humans allow flawed stories of the past to shape our views of the world and our expectations for the future. All of us continuously try to "make sense of the world." This is our consciousness at work. Because that process is so difficult and time-consuming, explanatory stories that people find compelling are simple rather than complex, concrete rather than abstract, assign a larger role to talent or lack of it, put greater stock in intelligence or lack of it; and credit intentions rather than luck for outcomes.[37] We all know how important it is to catch a bit of luck in litigation—serendipity, favorable timing—yet we often discount luck as a factor in how our cases turn out for our clients.

Our System 1 self quickly constructs a story based on whatever information we have at hand to explain the situation we confront. We develop a subjective confidence in our opinions to reflect the coherence of a story we have constructed, regardless of the small amount and low quality of the evidence on which we constructed the story.

We tend to focus on a few striking events that happened to catch our attention, rather than on the countless events that failed to happen.[38] We ignore base rates—facts about a population to which a case belongs—in making judgments about an event. We allow our subjective confidence in our own opinions to determine our assessment of the plausibility and strength of the story we have constructed, regardless of the small amount and low quality of the evidence on which that story is constructed,[39] often allowing inconsistency in making quick interpretations of and judgments about complex information.[40]

- One of the most well-known examples of the narrative fallacy is the legend of a six-year-old George Washington cutting down his father's cherry tree with a hatchet. The story is told to show President Washington's courage, honesty, and forthrightness: "I cannot tell a lie, I did cut it with my hatchet." This story was created by author Mason Weems, an early Washington biographer, to present the first president as an exemplary role model

[37] Kahneman, *supra* at 199–200. Recall that this was one of the observations discussed in Chapter 2 when we explored the power of the story form in litigation.

[38] *Id.* at 199 ("narrative fallacies").

[39] *Id.* at 209 ("confidence by coherence").

[40] *Id.* at 224–25.

for others. The story was never verified, but that didn't prevent the narrative from passing into the national consciousness.

- Our tendency to evaluate everything about another person positively or negatively based upon limited initial information is commonly referred to as the halo effect.[41] Dr. Kahneman describes this effect as "exaggerated emotional coherence" because our System 1 mode wants to simplify how we view people and situations. If we have a positive view of an expert witness we have used in the past, for example, we're less likely to ask hard questions about their credentials or the bases for their opinions in the present case, especially if they support the position our client wishes to take. The expert becomes an important character in the story we weave, even if his opinions might be suspect in the pending case.
- Disregard of base rates in constructing a story is commonplace in product liability litigation. A frequent case theme is: "This was an accident just waiting to happen. The product contained a fatal design flaw that was destined to cause this accident." A useful exercise in responding to this story would be to establish a base rate for the frequency of similar accidents. How many units of the product were on the market? Over what period were they in service? How many accidents occurred involving the product? What caused the accidents that did occur?
- Narratives, like viruses, can develop momentum in their power and quickly spread. A recent example of how a story line can shape not only public perception but behavior as well is George Floyd's death at the hands of the Minneapolis police. A vivid representation of police brutality in the form of a video showing a policeman kneeling on Mr. Floyd's neck until he died led to riots and demonstrations, greater distrust of police departments across the nation, and efforts in some jurisdictions to "defund" the police. The saliency of the visual images acted upon a society already raw from the COVID 19 pandemic to propel a powerful narrative.[42]

---

[41] *Id.* at 82–83 ("the halo effect").

[42] *See* Shiller *supra* at 53–68.

℞ – Ask: How do I know this narrative is factually accurate? What other sources of evidence are available about my subject? Am I just relying on my own initial view? How often does a particular event occur? What is the base rate for the event? Why did this specific event occur? What other evidence is there that puts this story in context?

[I] #9—Illusory Correlation

We fall into this mental trap when we leap to conclusions about relationship between two variables when none exists. Stereotyping is a potent form of illusory correlation. Stereotyping motivates a person to prefer appealing causal explanations for an event rather than to consider statistics that should persuade the person to modify or reject these causal explanations. Confusing temporal relationship with causal relationship is yet another. *Post hoc ergo propter hoc* is the classic formulation. Even though lawyers are trained to think logically about causes and effects, we can still fall prey to this logic trap. A few examples may illustrate this point.

- First, a silly example to help make the point using the *post hoc ergo propter hoc* fallacy. This is the logic trap that might assume trailer parks cause tornados, because every time you watch the news about a tornado touching down somewhere, you see footage of a wrecked trailer park.
- We frequently see illusory correlation at play in injury cases where a symptom or illness follows an event and the claim is made that the two not only are temporally related (one followed the other in time), but causally related (one caused the other) as well.
- During jury selection, I've watched senior trial lawyers fall back on gender, racial, or ethnic stereotypes to determine who they would strike from the jury. Instead of using specific attitudes, values, and beliefs described by a prospective juror in *voir dire* that might cause a juror to be favorably or unfavorably disposed to their specific case, they relied on "conventional wisdom" about the proclivities of jurors with certain characteristics they may have observed in other cases. "I'm going to strike that nurse. She treats injured people for a living and is likely to be

a sympathetic nurturer. And besides, she's Filipino American and Filipino women tend to be very tender hearted."

℞ – Ask: What is the causal relationship between Event A and Outcome B? And how do we know that? Is it a temporally related phenomenon or a causally related occurrence.

[J] #10—Assumptions About Witness Reliability

Jurors tend to credit the testimony of direct witnesses to events, conversations, and transactions because the person "was actually there" and "saw and heard things with their own eyes and ears." However, Professor Elizabeth Loftus has proved, through both substantial empirical studies and analyses of real-world events, that the reliability of all human beings' real-time perception of events they see and hear is far poorer than the general population thinks it is.[43] Eyewitnesses' mental processing and storage of what they think they have seen and heard, and their mental processing in later retrieving from memory and describing what they think they saw and heard, makes their testimony even more unreliable.

This is so for many reasons, including things occurring after a witnessed event can distort memory of that event, and that a witness's own internal thoughts, wishes, and desires intrude into the witness's memory.[44] People have a remarkable tendency to "see" what they want to see, regardless of whether what is in front of them is, for example, an unfolding auto accident, a video of an accident, or written records pertaining to an accident that they saw happen a week earlier. Consider these examples.

- An eyewitness to a police arrest of a burglary suspect is interviewed by an arresting officer and a statement is taken. The witness wants to be of assistance to the officers. Later, the witness is asked to testify about what he saw during the arrest. In preparation for his testimony, he gives a story that is at odds with his statement. He is shown his statement to refresh his recollection. This is a partial but incomplete help. He is then shown video of the arrest from a police camera to aid his

---

[43] Elizabeth F. Loftus, James M. Doyle, & Jennifer E. Dysart, *Eyewitness Testimony: Civil and Criminal* (5th ed. 2013).

[44] Elizabeth F. Loftus & Geoffrey F. Loftus, *On the Permanence of Stored Information in the Human Brain*, 35(5) Am. Psychol. 409–20 (May 1980).

recollection. What is the witness's true recollection, and what is constructed from the prior statement or the video?

- This same phenomenon affects a lawyer's interactions with others, including clients and counsel. Lawyers are "eyewitnesses" to what they think they are seeing and hearing. Our memories aren't perfect by a long shot. Our attention may fade in and out. We may have conveniently repackaged a memory to conform to a preferred perception of ourselves, what we said, or what we did. What is the validity of a recollection if it is offered by a distracted, incomplete, or self-serving reporter?

℞ – Ask: How do we know what we think we know? Did we hear or see what we thought we heard or saw? Are we safe in relying on our own perceptions in making decisions in the case? Are there contemporaneous recordings that can aid us in our recollection of events?

To avoid these decision-making traps, many of which come into play in litigation as you can see, we must discipline our intuition. How do we do that, albeit with great difficulty?

- Beware of creating System 1 stories.
- Place events in context to avoid narrow focus.
- Seek external data.
- Attend to the quality or lack of evidence; discount untrustworthy evidence.
- Focus on base rates.

The decision-making challenges, myths, and mental traps I've highlighted are common in complex litigation, but this list unfortunately is not exhaustive. There are many more. And you may have gathered by now that I've fallen prey to many of these at one point or another in my practice. I hope by sharing these with you and suggesting some prescriptions for avoiding or dealing with them, you and your clients can learn by reading about them rather than experiencing them. The quotation from Eleanor Roosevelt that began the introduction to this book is apt: "Learn from the mistakes of others. You can't live long enough to make them all yourself."

CHAPTER 6

THE BIG "TAKE AWAYS"

"If you can't explain something simply, you don't understand it well enough."

—Attributed to Albert Einstein

§ 6.01 UNDERSTANDING CLIENT OBJECTIVES

Effective representation begins with a thorough understanding of the client's objectives and priorities. Ask the client these questions.

- "What do you want?"
- "What does success look like?"
- "What are the financial and operational drivers behind this litigation?"

Then feed back to the client what you think you are hearing so there is no misunderstanding. Periodically repeat this conversation to see if the answers change, and with it your objectives. Here are some tips for effective client communication and relationships:

✔ Manage client expectations at the outset of the case. Inflated expectations of what is possible in litigation can lead to disappointment with the litigation team in spite of good results under the circumstances. Have a candid conversation about what is possible and what is not. Don't overpromise.

✔ Be prepared to balance the voice of the passionate advocate with the voice of the dispassionate advisor. The clients should know you're solidly in their corner and prepared to vigorously advocate for their position. But clients also need to know you'll give them an objective view of their case and a candid assessment of their options. Let the clients know which "voice" they are hearing as you communicate with them about their case.

✔ Be sensitive to the key client value drivers that will influence how litigation tradeoffs are made. You must not only be a good lawyer but also a savvy businessperson to be an effective team leader. Make it a point to understand business concerns that come into play in the litigation so that you don't lose sight of the operational drivers that influence how the clients' cases should be handled.

✔ Set client communication patterns so that the decision makers within your client's organization are kept informed.

✔ Develop a plan for initial crisis management and public messaging. Get your client's story out early. Consistently focus on and emphasize the client's story in communications with the media, your opponent, and the court.

- ✓ Prepare an initial case assessment that sets the initial plan for the case. The initial assessment and strategy will be your team's "mission." Pair the case assessment with a strategic budget that forecasts litigation costs. Use a spreadsheet to detail the anticipated tasks by phase of litigation, the hours anticipated to be devoted to each task, and the associated cost.
- ✓ Use litigation risk assessment tools such as decision trees to examine litigation variables that affect case value. Use the risk assessment as a tool to communicate possible pathways the case may follow, the probabilities and payoffs associated with the various pathways, and the costs and rewards of the litigation. I was cautious in the use of decision trees to stress to the client that while the valuations of outcomes, probabilities assigned to the occurrence of events, and overall presentation of the information gave a certain aura of mathematical certainty, litigation simply doesn't lend itself to that type of predictive precision. This is true particularly when paired with budgets, which by their very nature are cost estimates. Nevertheless, decision trees can help to define and quantify the risks faced by the client in the litigation.
- ✓ Take advantage of key client communication opportunities at inflection points in the litigation to brief the client on the status of the case.
- ✓ Remember that it isn't about the lawyers, it's about the case and the client. Don't let the litigation tail wag the company dog.

§ 6.02 STORYTELLING: THE ART OF THE ADVOCATE

Storytelling is the original form of human thought and communication. Our minds are hardwired to hear and respond to stories. Tap into the way people naturally think to advance your client's interests.

- ✓ Tell your client's story at every step in the litigation. Don't miss opportunities in early appearances before the court to communicate your client's narrative. Let the jury know in *voir dire* and opening why your client's story is to be preferred.

With each witness, lay out the elements of your client's story. Then tie a bow on the package with a closing that brings the facts together in a cohesive whole.

- ✓ Early in the case, develop a theory (a legal peg on which the case hangs) and theme (a universal principle) that defines your case. Pay attention to the characters and their motives in developing the proof of each element of your client's case. Spell out the plot (the sequence of events and interplay of characters and documents) in a way that is easily followed. Give the judge and jury the moral hook necessary to right a specific wrong in your client's favor.
- ✓ Test the potency of your story by asking if it fits the facts well, offers a satisfying explanation for how things happened, engages the listener, sets out a workable principle, and is easily understood.
- ✓ Make use of the visual dimension in telling your story. Remember that a vast majority of the population needs to *see* in order to believe.
- ✓ As you tell your client's story, remember to use your body to communicate nonverbally. Use your voice to create interest by varying tone, speed, and volume in your delivery.

§ 6.03 LEADING THE TEAM

Litigation leadership is the art of encouraging, influencing, and directing your team members to accomplish the objectives your client seeks to attain. There are five key behaviors that will make you a strong leader.

- ✓ *Integrity*—Litigation teams need to trust their leader. Create trust by speaking the truth, doing the right things, and respecting others. These are the badges of integrity. Model for the team the highest standards of professional conduct.
- ✓ *Courage*—Stay calm (or at least appear calm) in the face of changing circumstances. Remember that a duck looks calm on the surface of the water even when it is paddling like hell underneath the surface. Chart a course through ambiguous situations even when you don't have perfect information.

Hold yourself and your team accountable for results. Don't avoid the hard conversations.

- ✓ *Vision*—Create with your team a plan to win—a "roadmap to victory." Communicate that plan and the strategic intent behind it to your team. Changes in circumstances will require changes in the plan, so fearlessly adapt, adjust, and overcome when a new plan is required.
- ✓ *Team Building*—Instill in your team a belief they are part of an organization defined by integrity, service, and professional excellence. Select team members with differing skill sets that equip the entire team to accomplish the client's objectives. Demand that team members check their egos at the door. Invest in your team through training and mentoring so they grow professionally and personally.
- ✓ *Resilience*—You must exhibit persistence in pursuing team objectives. Build esprit de corps so that each member lifts others around them. Embed a culture of continuous improvement and an attitude that when failure occurs, team members will "fail forward," learning from their mistakes.

§ 6.04 MANAGING THE CASE

Litigation has much in common with other complex processes in that effective management can affect how smoothly and efficiently the process unfolds. Follow the project management process. Define objectives, identify and assign tasks necessary to accomplish the objectives, then monitor and control the execution of the tasks to maintain quality and control costs.

- ✓ Prepare the case as if you are preparing for trial. At the outset of the case, create a trial notebook that collects in digital form or in a series of binders all the information or materials necessary to walk into a courtroom and try a case.
- ✓ Create digital shared workspaces for document production and review, and trial exhibit preparation. A shared workspace is also helpful for collection of case materials and task lists.
- ✓ Create and maintain a task list that spells out what will be done, who will do it, when it will be done, and the status of

each task. Give guidance to the person responsible for a task regarding how much time should be invested in the accomplishment of the task.

- ✔ Staff leanly and avoid team turnover. This will give team members a chance to stretch and grow and will redound to the benefit of the client in reduced costs.
- ✔ Eliminate bottlenecks in work processes and work product review. Delegate so that you don't become the bottleneck.

§ 6.05 LITIGATION DECISION MAKING

There are a lot of myths out there about how humans make decisions. Don't buy into them. Appreciate that there are limits to how logically and dispassionately humans make decisions.

- ✔ Humans aren't perfectly rational actors.
- ✔ We aren't always good users of data. And we don't always bring analytical rigor to our decision making.
- ✔ We often let emotions enter and rule our decision making.
- ✔ We assume that because we're pretty smart cookies, we are immune from making bad choices.
- ✔ We look to the team leader as the person who makes decisions, and don't appreciate that each member of the team has a role to play in the decision-making process.
- ✔ We can't expect the decision process to unfold in a perfectly linear way. Real life isn't like that. More often, decisions are made in an iterative process that proceeds in fits and starts by trying something to see if it works, then doing something else to see if another approach works better.
- ✔ Avoid common decision-making traps by watching for biases and fallacies in our thinking, then asking some basic questions that will steer your team around the trap. Listed below are some of the more common traps encountered in litigation.
- ✔ *Base rate errors* come from ignoring the broader population from which a sample is drawn. Ask if you're making judgments based on a plausible base rate.

- ✔ *Overconfidence bias* creeps into decision making when we look at the world through the proverbial rose-colored glasses. Simply asking what could go wrong, and if so, at what cost will help avoid this trap.
- ✔ When you double down on past investments or prior decisions without looking at the returns on the next dollar invested, you abandon sound incremental thinking. To avoid the *sunk cost effect*, focus on the costs and rewards of the next action your team might take.
- ✔ You can lose perspective if you rely only on the most readily available information—the *availability bias*—in making decisions. To avoid this trap, ask what other information is available to inform your team's judgment, even if it is more difficult or time-consuming to gather.
- ✔ All of us are prone to gathering and relying on information that confirms our existing viewpoint, the *confirmation bias*. You need a "devil's advocate" to ask the hard questions about the information you choose to rely upon the analysis you develop based on that information.
- ✔ Be suspicious of initial reference points that can distort our estimates, particularly when they are arbitrary or don't appear to be well grounded. If you ask what the relevance of the initial reference point is, the *anchoring effect* at play will become obvious. Then you can decide how to counter it.
- ✔ People often look for causal explanations for events even where there isn't one. To avoid the *illusory correlation effect*, you should ask whether the correlation is causal or temporal, and how you know that. Look for false cause and effect correlations.
- ✔ *Framing biases* come from mental models we all carry around in our heads and use to understand the world. How you frame a question often determines the answer. You need to observe how the question to be decided is framed, and ask whether there are other frames that might yield a different answer.
- ✔ You fall prey to the *substitution effect* when you unconsciously answer a simpler question than the harder question that was asked. As trial lawyers, we recognize non-responsive

answers to questions. You need to call yourself on the substitution when you engage in it.

- ✔ People routinely make *assumptions about human nature* that may be based on stereotypes. If you ask whether you are generalizing about people and how those views shape your decision making, you can identify this pitfall in thinking.
- ✔ We make *assumptions about the reliability of observations and memory*, both for ourselves and for others. Be very careful in crediting memory unaided by contemporaneous documents. Ask the basic "what do I know and why do I think I know it" question to avoid this potential trap.
- ✔ We latch onto stories of the past that shape our view of the world without questioning the ongoing accuracy of those stories. You can avoid problems created by the *narrative fallacy* by questioning why an event occurred and how often it occurs.
- ✔ Logical fallacies also can take us down the wrong road in our thinking. Watch out for *appeals to tradition* that say "we've always done it this way" when a new approach is needed. Be wary of the *slippery slope* argument that resists logical dividing lines. Define terms carefully to avoid *equivocation* that can lead to muddy exchanges.

Have your antennae out to spot those pesky biases and fallacies that harm the effectiveness of our decision making. Remember to name the bias or fallacy at play, and deconstruct it to get back on the path to sound decision making.

You continuously will be called upon as the team leader to lead group decision-making exercises or as a valued team member to participate in decision-making processes. As a team leader, create the conditions that will produce good decisions. This means getting the right people together in the right environment with the right resources to produce a dialog where the wisdom and thinking of the best informed and most knowledgeable emerges. As a team member, respectfully contribute your viewpoint when you can provide valuable information and perspective. Discussions of this type are the hallmark of effective teams, and will produce the best results for your clients.

§ 6.06 FINAL THOUGHTS

I hope that this book will prove helpful to you in navigating the reefs and sand bars of complex litigation as such cases become ever more complex, demanding, and globally interconnected. Bet the company litigation places great demands on both team leaders and team members. Service as national trial and coordinating counsel for clients faced with complex litigation is one of the hardest things to do, and do well. My wish is that the information I've shared with you in this book, and that I often learned the hard way, will be useful to you in your practice. Perfection may be unattainable, but improvement is always possible.

BIBLIOGRAPHY

"So many books, so little time."

—Frank Zappa

Manual for Complex Litigation (Fourth) (2004).

Michael E. Tigar, *Examining Witnesses* (2nd ed. 2004).

Michael E. Tigar, *Persuasion: The Litigator's Art* (1999).

Irving Younger, *The Advocate's Deskbook: The Essentials of Trying a Case* (1988).

Gerry Spence, *How to Argue and Win Every Time* (1995).

Stephen Lubet, *Modern Trial Advocacy—Analysis and Practice* (2nd ed. 1997).

Keith Evans, *Common Sense Rules of Advocacy for Lawyers* (2004).

Hon. John F. Nangle, *From the Horse's Mouth: The Workings of the Judicial Panel on Multidistrict Litigation*, 66 Def. Couns. J. 341 (1999).

Don G. Rushing & Ellen N. Adler, *Some Inconvenient Truths About Forum Non Conveniens Law in International Aviation Disasters*, 74 J. Air L. & Com. 403 (2009).

David E. Steinberg, *Motion to Transfer and the Interests of Justice*, 66 Notre Dame L. Rev. 443 (1999).

Jay Tidmarsh & Roger H. Trangsrud, *Complex Litigation and Its Alternatives* (Foundation Press 2002).

John Locke, *An Essay Concerning Human Understanding Book III* (Kenneth P. Winkler ed. 1996).

Elizabeth F. Loftus & Geoffrey R. Loftus, *On the Permanence of Stored Information in the Brain*, 35(5) Am. Psychol. 409–20 (May 1980).

Elizabeth F. Loftus, David G. Miller, & Helen J. Burns, *Semantic Integration of Verbal Information into a Visual Memory*, 4(1) J. Exp. Psychol. Hum. Learn. Mem. 19–31 (1978).

Norman R. Augustine, *Managing the Crisis You Tried to Prevent*, Harvard Business Review (November/December 1995).

Thomas L. Sager, Julie S. Mazza, *The Competitive Edge—The Growing Power of the DuPont Legal Model* (4th ed.).

DuPont Legal Department, *Leaps & Bounds—Moving Ahead with the DuPont Legal Mode*l (Crosby Marketing 2001).

Burton Marcus *et al.*, *Mathematics for Marketing—Decision Trees*, Modern Marketing 721 (1975).

Paul Slovic, Baruch Fischhoff, & Sarah Lichtenstein, *Response Mode, Framing and Information Processing Effects in Risk Assessment*, New Directions for Methodology of Social and Behavioral Science: Question Framing and Response Consistency 21–36 (Robin Hogarth ed. 1982).

Frank H. Knight, *Risk, Uncertainty and Profit* 197 *et seq.* (2006).

Bruce Caldwell, *Ten (Mostly) Hayekian Insights for Trying Economic Times*, (2011).

Don G. Rushing, *Storytelling: The Art of the Advocate,* 49 ABA Litig. J. No. 3 16, (Spring 2023).

Philip N. Meyer, *Storytelling for Lawyers* (2014).

Gerry L. Spence, *Story Telling,* 72 ABA J. Lawyer's Magazine 63 (Apr. 1, 1986).

Daniel Kahneman, *Thinking, Fast and Slow* (2011).

Edmund T. Rolls, *The Cingulate Cortex and Limbic Systems for Emotion, Action, and Memory,* Brain Structure & Function 224 (2019).

Peter M. Vishton, *Understanding the Secrets of Human Perception* (2011).

Henri J. M. Nouwen, *The Living Reminder* (2009).

John Steinbeck, *East of Eden* (1952).

Thomas S. Kuhn, *The Structure of Scientific Revolutions* (3rd ed. 1996).

Robert M. Pirsig, *Zen and the Art of Motorcycle Maintenance—An Inquiry into Values* 70–72 (2005).

Gerry Spence, *Win Your Case* (2005).

Keith Evans, *Common* Sense Rules of Advocacy for Lawyers (2004)

Keith Evans, *The Golden Rules of Advocacy* 66 (1993).

James W. McElhaney, *From Start to Finish*, Am. Bar Ass'n J. 52–53 (Oct. 2000).

James T. Hall, *Practically Profound: Putting Philosophy to Work in Everyday Life* (2005).

Harold Pashler, Douglas Rohrer, & Robert Bjork, *Learning Styles: Concepts and Evidence,* 9.3 Psychol. Sci. Pub. Int. 103–19 (2008).

Paul A. Kirschner, *Stop Propagating the Learning Styles Myth*, 106 Comput. & Educ. 166–71 (2017).

William C. Bradford, *Reaching the Visual Learner: Teaching Property Through Art*, 11 The Law Teacher (2004).

Regine Zopf, Claire Marie Giabbiconi, Thomas Gruber, & Matthias M. Müller, *Attentional Modulation of the Human Somatosensory Evoked Potential in a Trial-by-trial Spatial Cueing and Sustained Spatial Attention Task Measured with High Density 128 channels EEG*, 20 *Brain Research, Cognitive Brain Research* 491–509 (2004).

Frank Coffield, David Moseley, Elaine Hall, & Kathryn Ecclestone, Learning Styles and Pedagogy in Post-16 Learning—A Systematic and Critical Review, London: Learning and Skills Research (2004).

Colin James, Miles Bore, & Susanna Zito, *Emotional Intelligence and Personality as Predictors of Psychological Well-being*, 30(4) J. Psychoeduc. Assess. 425–38 (2012).

John Gardner, *On Leadership* 6 (1990).

Leah W. Teague & Stephen L. Rispoli, *The Study of Leadership Theories: Great Leaders Are Made, Not Born*, American Bar Association Law Practice Magazine (November/December 2021).

Peter F. Drucker, *Management: Tasks, Responsibilities, Practices* (1974).

Kim Campbell, *Flying in the Face of Fear: A Fighter Pilot's Lessons in Leading with Courage* (2023).

Scott S. Barker, *Reflections on Trial Lawyer Leadership*, Colorado Lawyer (September 2023).

Fred Fiedler & Martin Chemers, *Leadership and Effective Management* (1974).

Dominic Scott & R. Edward Freeman, *Models of Leadership in Plato and Beyond* (2021).

James M. Burns, *Leadership* (1978).

James Collins, *Good to Great: Why Some Companies Make the Leap . . . and Others Don't* (2001).

Robert K. Greenleaf, *Servant Leadership—A Journey into the Nature of Legitimate Power and Greatness* (1977).

Jordan Lewis, *Trusted Partners* (1999).

Angela Duckworth, *Grit: The Power of Passion and Perseverance* (2016);

Samuel B. Griffith, *Sun Tzu—The Art of War* (1963).

Gary Hamel & C.K. Prahalad, *Strategic Intent*, Harvard Business Review (July-August 2005).

Stephen R. Covey, *The 7 Habits of Highly Effective People* (1989).

William H. McRaven, *Make Your Bed: Little Things That Can Change Your Life . . . And Maybe the World* (2017).

John Stuart Mill, *On Liberty & Utilitarianism* (1993).

Ken Blanchard & Spencer Johnston, *The One Minute Manager* (1986).

Tom Peters & Robert H. Waterman, Jr., *In Search of Excellence; Lessons from America's Best Run Companies* (1982).

Amy J.C. Cuddy, Matthew Kohut, & John Neffinger, *Connect, Then Lead*, Harvard Business Review (July-August 2013) (https://hbr.org/2013/07/connect-then-lead).

John Hagel III, *Good Leadership Is About Asking Good Questions*, Harvard Business Review (January 8, 2021).

Daniel H. Pink, *Drive—The Surprising Truth About What Motivates Us* (2011).

Brene Brown, *Dare to Lead* (2018).

Jim Mattis & Bing West, *Call Sign Chaos* 45 (2019).

Don G. Rushing & Andrew B. Serwin, *Pathways to Wellness in the Practice of Law,* The Bencher 24 (March/April 2020).

Anne Lamott, *Bird by Bird: Some Instructions on Writing and Life* (1994).

Irving Janis, *Groupthink* (1982).

Richard H. Thaler, *From Homo Economicus to Homo Sapiens*, 14(1) J. Econ. Perspect. 133–14 (2000).

Sharon Bertsch McGrayne, *The Theory That Would Not Die* (2011).

John B. Cobb, Jr. & David Ray Griffin, *Process Theology—an Introductory Exposition* (1976).

David Ronayne, Daniel Sgiori, & Anthony Tuckwell, *How Susceptible Are You to the Sunk Cost Fallacy?*, Harv. Bus. Rev. (July 15, 2021).

Daniel Kahneman & Amos Tversky, *Choices, Values, and Frames*, 34 Am. Psychol. (1984).

Don Rushing, Linda Lane, & Erin Bosman, *Anchors Away: Attacking Dollar Suggestions for Non-Economic Damages in Closing*, Def. Couns. J. 378–85 (July 2003).

Steven Pinker, *The Better Angels of Our Nature* (2012).

Garrison Keillor, *The Keillor Reader* (2014).

John Krakauer, *Up Into Thin Air* (1997).

Matthew Rabin & Richard Thaler, *Anomalies—Risk Aversion*, 15(1) J. Econ. Perspect. 226 (Winter 2001).

Robert J. Shiller, *Narrative Economics—How Stories Go Viral & Drive Major Economic Events* (2019).

Elizabeth F. Loftus, James M. Doyle, & Jennifer E. Dysart, *Eyewitness Testimony: Civil and Criminal* (5th ed. 2013).

Elizabeth F. Loftus & Geoffrey F. Loftus, *On the Permanence of Stored Information in the Human Brain*, 35(5) Am. Psychol. 409–20 (May 1980).

INDEX

References are to sections.